Word Ways

WORD WAYS

The Novels of D'Arcy McNickle

John Lloyd Purdy

The University of Arizona Press, Tucson

The University of Arizona Press

Copyright © 1990
The Arizona Board of Regents
All Rights Reserved

This book was set in Linotron 202 Meridien.
∞ This book is printed on acid-free, archival-quality paper.
Manufactured in the United States of America.

94 93 92 91 90   5 4 3 2 1

Library of Congress Cataloging-in-Publication Data

Purdy, John Lloyd.
    Word ways : the novels of D'Arcy McNickle / John Lloyd Purdy.
       p.   cm.
    Includes bibliographical references (p.   ).
    ISBN 0-8165-1157-8 (alk. paper)
    1. McNickle, D'Arcy, 1904–1977—Criticism and interpretation.
2. Indians in literature. I. Title.
PS3525.A2844Z84   1990
813'.52—dc20   89-27106
                                                          CIP

British Library Cataloguing in Publication data are available.

Frontispiece: Photograph of D'Arcy McNickle,
courtesy of The Newberry Library, Chicago, Illinois.

Dedicated to the memory of D'Arcy McNickle
and to the efforts of those who work
to keep the stories alive,
and to my son Carl, who was born
with *Word Ways* and who was always
willing to listen to it change

Contents

Acknowledgments

I would like to thank those who read and responded to the early drafts of this book. In particular, I thank Kathleen Sands, Marvin Fisher, Kenneth Morrison, Elizabeth Brandt, and Wilfred Ferrell, whose encouragement and insights are greatly appreciated. Finally, I want to thank the directors of the Newberry Library for allowing me access to McNickle's personal papers and for funding my stay at the library with a fellowship. I am specifically indebted to Richard Brown, whose kindness went beyond his required duties and who shared his memories of McNickle to help me see the man behind the writings.

JOHN LLOYD PURDY

Introduction

D'Arcy McNickle spent his adult life in the mainstream of Euramerican society, far removed from the reservation of his youth. In this urbane environment, his ability to gain knowledge of and insights about American culture became his means of survival and his pathway to success. For over five decades he carved a reputation for himself that crossed the line not only between several occupations but also between cultures. He was an anthropologist but also a writer of fiction, a bureaucrat but also a historian, a political activist but also a poet. From this perspective, his personal history seems to suggest that he had become a perfect example of the assimilated Indian. The forces of Euramerican society appear to have succeeded in their attempts to make this one Indian forget his heritage and conform to a new set of cultural ideals.

The propensity to consider only two possible "types" of Indians—"traditional" or "modern"—is indeed strong, as is the desire to look at an individual as representative of all Native cultures (or, as it is often phrased, "culture," with its implication of a monolithic rather than a pluralistic perception). However, such dichotomies are as limited as the "good Indian/dead Indian" of Hollywood fame. Like all living cultures, those of the Native Americans are in constant flux, which forces individuals to contend with new, often dangerous, circumstances. Indeed, McNickle's life story spans six decades during which Native cultures faced momentous threats to their existence, including the federal "termination" policies of the 1950s. But these were also decades that saw the emergence of a continent-wide renewal of Native consciousness, a sense of pride and power based upon, but not always coincidental with, earlier tribal values and beliefs. McNickle's novels have this renewal as their subject, and the story of how he wrote them is the story of Native Americans in this century as they addressed sweeping changes in their world and simultaneously reaffirmed tribal identity.

Although he is not wholly representative, McNickle's life and works provide invaluable insights into these decades of change, as well as into the evolution of a distinct body of narrative, termed, for lack of a better title, contemporary Native American fiction. As a bureaucrat, McNickle supported the sovereignty of ancient tribal ways of government and the formulation of federal policies that employ traditional tribal power structures rather than those arbitrarily imposed by nontribal politicians. As an anthropologist, he championed the "scientific" study of Native cultures. And as a writer, he brought his knowledge of Western European and American literary conventions together with his experiences as a boy growing up on the reservation, thus creating a hybrid: the modern, American/Indian novel. His contributions in the area of government and Indian relations are a matter of record, and they are highly regarded; his efforts in anthropology have long been recognized, and his death sadly noted by his colleagues in that field; but his innovations in the area of fiction have never been adequately explored or acknowledged.

McNickle's first novel was published in 1936. Like so many other Indian works of his time and later, his fiction focuses on Native subjects and, ironically, is therefore in peril of falling victim to one of two equally tragic fates. It could easily be lost in the never-ending avalanche of works *about* Indians written *by* Anglos: romanticized works of fiction or "history," usually unworthy of attention by the reader interested in veracity. But because his fiction varies from this popular genre in its handling of the subject matter, it risks never attaining the popularity enjoyed by the romanticized accounts of Indian life. McNickle's first novel dropped immediately into obscurity while, a few years earlier, a novel about Indians written by an Anglo, Oliver La Farge's *Laughing Boy*, won the Pulitzer Prize. Fortunately, things have changed somewhat since 1936.

Until recently, interest in things Indian has been limited either to a slim, informed section of American scholarly circles or to a cult of the fashionable, both of which provide a very narrow readership. Within the last fifteen years, the study of Native literatures has mushroomed. A vast field of scholarly endeavor has resulted, and

McNickle's popularity has benefited from the increased attention. In fact, all his novels have been rereleased recently. If one considers the innovations that he brought to his novels, the mythic quality of their narratives, and their thematic complexity and potential for multi-leveled interpretation, the lack of attention his work has received to date is incomprehensible. McNickle became adept at adapting the novel to his purpose, a purpose very similar to those of Indian writers who have followed.

The decisions and choices he made as an author—a novelist in the American literary tradition—came to him from two sources that at first appear incompatible. His power as a writer came when he shed his attempts to write fiction in keeping solely with the styles and concerns of other contemporary American novelists. Instead, he used tribal verbal arts to shape his writing, thus giving his works an engaging quality that marks them as distinctive but also as precursory of more recent works by American Indian novelists. McNickle intended his works to be statements of the ability of Native cultures to endure despite consistent, and sometimes violent, efforts to destroy them. The theme of survival is apparent to readers who drop their preconceived notions about the demise of Native peoples and cultures and allow the narratives to move them in ways strongly reminiscent of tribal narratives.

The following study charts McNickle's growth as a writer of fiction and examines the ways by which he hoped to educate through his writings. It focuses primarily on his three novels: *The Surrounded, Runner in the Sun: A Story of Indian Maize,* and *Wind from an Enemy Sky.* His first and his last novels are particularly significant in that they date from the same era—the 1930s—but *Wind* underwent, literally, decades of revision and reflection before its publication in 1978, the year following McNickle's death. It reflects both the continued refinement of his perception of Native cultures, his awareness of what Kenneth Lincoln has called the "renaissance of American Indian literature," and his acknowledgment that his audience's awareness had indeed changed over the forty years that separate the novel's birth and its publication. Each of the novels demonstrates his role as a storyteller in a sense very similar to that of a tribal storyteller, whose purpose is to entertain but also to enlighten.

In McNickle's hands, the novel provides significant insights into Native cultures in general, but also into specific ways of gaining the knowledge of how to endure difficult times. McNickle also shows how humankind may endure, and perhaps prevail, in the phrase of his contemporary, William Faulkner. In traditional Native verbal arts, audiences are shown how this knowledge is sometimes derived directly from the environment through a vision quest, a tradition that has a wide distribution throughout Native cultures on this continent and that is widely used as a structural device in novels about them. At its basis, the vision quest is a journey of education, a search for ways to act or react, and as such it is a logical stucturing device for a study of McNickle's evolution as a novelist as well. Like a Salish/Cree man seeking knowledge, McNickle lived through a time of deprivation, set out on a search for understanding, and was rewarded with some lasting insights into Native cultures that became the bases of his novels and contributions toward the survival of those cultures. And like a visionary in the Salish/Cree traditions, he reached this insight while in voluntary isolation from his family and their land. In fact, the irony of McNickle's life may be that his vision came while he was actively engaged in mainstream American society, which was bent on the obliteration of Indian cultures, and while he lived in urban settings remarkably different from those of his home.

Word Ways

1 The Initiation:
Fasting and Setting Out

The highway north out of Missoula, Montana, climbs through the steep foothills that mark the southern boundary of the Flathead Indian Reservation. It is a rough road, pitted and scarred by the harsh winters that are a part of life in that land. After it crosses the reservation boundary, the road briefly follows the Jocko River, the narrow stream that Father Jean De Smet followed in 1840 on his mission into the wilderness to save the Indians. As the road climbs the final ridge before St. Ignatius, its black surface blends into the dark, timbered peaks of the Mission Range several miles away. They are the uniform, awe-inspiring barrier of the reservation's eastern boundary. From the top of the ridge, one can see far to the north where the waters of Flathead Lake stretch for thirty miles along the north-south wall of the Missions. The lake, so one story goes, was created by a monstrous flood that covered the low hills and valleys, killing nearly all the Flathead Indians or, as they may be more accurately called, the Salish. Only a few were saved by one man who, calling upon his guardian spirit, shot arrows at the rising water until it stopped—and then receded.[1] His people survive because he persevered against a seemingly irresistible force.

To the west, the Bitterroot Mountains are a blue haze in the distance. These are, most likely, the guides the Salish followed on their migration to this land from the Pacific Northwest coast, where their kinsmen in the Salishan language family still live today. Far to the south is the Ram's Horn Tree, a place where people may gain power to overcome adversity. Here Sinchlep, the Salish culture hero, is said to have defeated an evil adversary through faith in his power and by his own quick wit. To the east are the trails the Salish once traveled to the plains to hunt buffalo, and sometimes to fight their traditional enemies, the Blackfeet. Below, the old Catholic mission of St. Ignatius stands as it has for nearly a century and a half, an obstinate monument dwarfed by its surroundings. This is the valley of *Sniel-emen*, the valley of the surrounded.

Forty-five years after De Smet's arrival, Isidore Plante Parenteau and his family followed the Missions into the valley. Like many of his kinsmen, he had participated in the Northwest Rebellion in the Saskatchewan Territory, sometimes referred to as the Riel Rebellion after Louis Riel who led the Métis in their attempt to block the loss of their homelands to immigrants from the east. Descendants of Cree Indians and white French trappers, the Métis saw the Hudson's Bay Company's sale of the northwest territory to the Canadian government as a threat to their livelihood and traditions. When men arrived to survey the land and plot it into sections for homesteading and sale, the Métis reacted violently. The hostilities lasted sixteen years, despite temporary truces and short-lived resolutions of the conflict. Finally, in 1885, Riel was captured, tried, and hanged for his part in the rebellion. The war lost, many of the Métis fled southward into the United States, living as best they could and wandering from reservation to reservation until those who remained were granted their own lands after the turn of the century. Others, such as Parenteau and his family, were adopted by their host tribes. As a result of their acceptance by the Salish, his daughter, Philomene, was alloted eighty acres of farmland, as was each of her three children, Ruth, Florence, and D'Arcy.

Daughter of a Métis leader and wife of an Anglo farmer, Philomene lived a life in which calls for conformity, and therefore conflict, were constant. Once the Métis roamed freely through their land; now they were outcasts restricted to narrow, unfamiliar places designated as "reservations" by the U.S. federal government. Even more vexing, she and her once powerful people were dependent upon the charity and tolerance of others. Plunged into a new place and lifeway, she had little control over her own fate—yet she bore and raised three children and ultimately became a property owner in her new land. Although she was at the mercy of social, economic, and governmental forces she could little comprehend, she fought a furious battle to maintain custody of her children and their lands after her divorce from William McNickle. Hers was a life of accommodation, if not resignation.

On the eighth day of April 1913, Philomene wrote a letter to Superior Court in St. Ignatius, Montana. In it, she tried to exercise her rights as a member of the Confederated Flathead and Kootenai tribes. Her estranged husband, William McNickle, had been granted management of their children's land allotments, even though the land was deeded to them as a result of Philomene's adoption into the tribe and he was not a tribal member. Her letter, which was riddled with misspelled words, poor grammar, and slang, did not right the wrong; her children's lands, and their futures, had been appropriated.

During the ensuing divorce proceedings, she wrote another impassioned plea to the court, in which she begged that her son, D'Arcy McNickle, be allowed to remain with her; the court had ruled earlier that he was to be sent to Chemawa Indian School. Again her request was denied. When the time came for the boy to leave, he mysteriously disappeared from the train station, and Philomene and her new husband, Gus Dahlberg, were arrested for kidnapping. Philomene claimed that the boy had run away of his own accord because he did not want to leave his family and friends to travel the hundreds of miles to Oregon and school. Owing to lack of evidence, she and Gus were finally released, and Philomene's education in the ways of power in white society had reached a crucial juncture.[2]

Like all Native American peoples since the incursion of the European, Philomene and her generation had to confront powerful forces working to dominate and direct them. Euramerican society was set on the assimilation of "The Vanishing Indian," and she seemed powerless to resist its influence. By October 22, 1914, her son's future was sealed. On that day, the Mother Superior of the Indian school in St. Ignatius wrote a letter to Agent Morgan of the Flathead Reservation in which she discussed Philomene's attempts to regain custody of D'Arcy, who was living with his father at the time: "We fear the mother's influence would destry [*sic*] all our efforts towards the training of his character."[3] The forces of conversion, bent upon the alteration of Native character, came close to their goal.

Despite his brief escape, McNickle was sent to Salem, Oregon, where he attended Chemawa, but the battle for "the training of his character" was far from over. In a letter to the Office of Indian Affairs in Washington, D.C., dated November 2, 1914, Philomene once again tried to sway the powers that wanted to shape her son's "character." However, this letter, which was obviously composed for her, was flawlessly organized and written, and in it she expressed her desire to raise young D'Arcy as a white man, not an "indian."[4] Philomene had learned from her past mistakes: she adopted her adversaries' rhetorical strategies (their own conventions of expression), as well as their perceptions of Native peoples in her attempt to achieve a just hearing. She recognized how important it was to understand white society's means of communication and the impressions they convey. In a word, she finally understood her audience: its strengths and its vulnerabilities. Although she was ultimately unsuccessful in keeping her son near her, she had held his future, briefly, in her words. Philomene's lesson was learned by her son also, but he came to it in a very different way.

D'Arcy McNickle was born in St. Ignatius on January 18, 1904. When he was of age, he attended the Catholic school at the mission, but his education had begun long before then. As he later recalled in a letter to Constance Skinner, the literary critic, "the stories and songs of those people [his Métis family and their Salish hosts] were the first I ever heard."[5] Like so many other Native American children, his first education came through verbal arts, an oral literary tradition. There is a great deal of debate concerning the extent of his participation, but there is little doubt that his life on the reservation led to memorable encounters with a lifeway guided by oral stories. However, his early education was soon challenged by that of the mission school, and of Chemawa, a federal Indian boarding school, where a conflicting set of cultural beliefs was imposed—that of the transplanted European.

There is little information about McNickle's years at the mission school or Chemawa, but the way that he describes the schools in his writings, in particular his novels, leaves little doubt about his judgment of his experiences in them; these memories did not evoke the nostalgia that the memories of the childhood songs and stories evoked. They were obviously trying times for him, as they were for other Indian children who had to live through the same ordeal. As McNickle was to write four decades later in *Indians and Other Ameri-*

cans: Two Ways of Life Meet, Indian boarding schools emphasized "military discipline and the complete regimentation of the child's waking hours. Moreover, the schools were dedicated to the complete eradication of all traits of Indian culture."[6] Children were often punished for misbehavior, which often meant non-Anglo behavior. They were also punished if caught speaking their native languages or practicing their peoples' customs—those basic, crucial actions that tied them to their people who were quite often far away. Isolation was the key:

> The first off-reservation boarding schools, Carlisle and Chemawa, were founded by army men encouraged by [Richard Henry] Pratt's successful experiences with Indian prisoners in Florida. Both were well away from reservations and were designed to remove their students from their homes and tribal cultures for extended periods of time so that they could be instilled with American values, culture, and aspirations.[7]

"American values, culture, and aspirations." Ironically, however, isolation is also a Salish and Cree tradition in education. Often, when a threat is perceived, the knowledge of how to address that threat is gained through vision quests that begin with one man's separation from his people but end with a new awareness of his relationship with and responsibilities to them. This is what happened to McNickle. Not only did his character survive the attempts to supplant his early education, but he appears to have flourished because of them.

In fact, he continued in the school system long after he was required to do so. He attended the University of Montana for over three years, where he majored in English literature and won a statewide poetry contest in 1925. At this time, a friend of his left to study at Oxford University. McNickle was anxious to follow, but he needed funds. Unfortunately, he possessed only one thing of value, a thing of supreme importance to his family and to his mother in particular. As he was to write later, "in my impatience I sold my land allotment. . . ."[8] He went to Oxford, but he did not take a degree because the university refused to transfer a sufficient number of credits from Montana. Thus, after a year at Oxford he moved to France for six months and then returned to the United States.

However, it would be years before he would return to the land he left through the sale of his allotment, and then only on a few, brief visits.

For someone who expressed in his fiction such nostalgia for the land and people of his birth and such distaste for his early experiences in the American school system, McNickle's accomplishments are quite impressive—and confusing. Like his mother and her people, he obviously possessed a powerful desire to move freely through the world, directing his own life as he went, and his accomplishments stand as tribute to his ability to learn and to implement the knowledge he gained about lifeways radically different from those of his family. On the surface, McNickle seems to have adopted fully the ways of life found in "mainstream" America, the "American values, culture, and aspirations" largely Anglo in origin. But one need not dig too deeply into McNickle's history and writings to find evidence that demonstrates the extent to which the cultures of his childhood (Cree and Métis, but also Salish) remained an inseparable part of his being, directing his values and aspirations throughout his life, although their influence was not manifested in any material way.

In 1979, Alfonso Ortiz wrote an obituary for McNickle that provides an insight into the motivations of his onetime mentor and longtime friend. In Ortiz's view, McNickle "observed that, despite what seemed on the surface to be massive and rapid breakdown in Indian cultures across the continent, an essential core of cultural integrity was being maintained."[9] For nearly four centuries, American society has held the view that Indian cultures are on the brink of oblivion; such a view led early anthropologists, as well as amateur ethnographers, hastily to record Native lifeways and oral literatures before they were lost. Such a view has formed many of the government's policies toward the Indians and has colored popular perception about the strengths, durability, and, therefore, "legitimacy" of Native cultures.[10] And this view was reinforced by literary works and character types from every era of American literature. From Freneau's "The Indian Burying Ground" to Faulkner's Sam Fathers, and from Cooper's *The Last of the Mohicans* to Kesey's "Chief" Bromden, Native societies and characters have been depicted as extinct or nearing extinction or (worse yet) assimilation. That is, until Mc-Nickle published his first novel.

McNickle recognized that Indian cultures survive, that they endure today despite repeated efforts to kill them. Something remains, as it always has, to guide and to ensure perpetuation of tribal identity, and McNickle's papers—housed in the Newberry Library in Chicago—offer constant support for Ortiz's insight, and evidence of McNickle's estimation of what constitutes the cultural "core" that has such a tenacious hold on life.

One piece of evidence is entitled "Memorandum for the Press." Written in the late 1930s while McNickle was on the staff of John Collier, the Commissioner of Indian Affairs, the lengthy article presents the information contained in a speech McNickle made to the Missouri Archaeological Society in Kansas City. Apparently, the press release was written by McNickle himself because, rather than summarize the highlights of the speech, it develops into a lengthy, persuasive retelling of it, complete with statistics and historical examples. The point of his speech is quite clear: Indian ceremonial practices and social organizations are still vital and active, despite appearances to the contrary. He writes:

> Actually, Indian life is far richer than most of us suspect. There was a time, not so long ago, when the Government officially frowned upon Indian ceremonialism. Orders were issued for the purpose of suppressing those ceremonies which were considered objectionable and of curtailing the practice of the simpler social forms of ceremony. As a result of such an official attitude, much of the Native ceremonial life disappeared; it did not necessarily come to an end, it may simply have gone underground. The Pueblo Indians of the Southwest, for example, learned at a comparatively early period in its [*sic*] relations with the white world to keep its own secrets, and today there are things about the Pueblo Indians of which we have not the least knowledge.[11]

He goes on to discuss, at length, traditional Creek Indian sociopolitical organizations that remain strong, even though the government had tried to supplant them with its own. He clearly states that Indian lifeways endure even though they may not be immediately recognizable. This is, of course, a generalization, but one that he obviously endorsed, and one cannot help but wonder if it may be equally applied to McNickle himself. Perhaps the cultural lifeways he experienced as a youth endured in him, even though they remained largely hidden, forced underground, by the nature and number of his accomplishments in Anglo society.

In his role as bureaucrat, as the tenor of his speech suggests, McNickle worked to educate the public and the government about the ways of Native cultures, their strengths as well as their needs. He also played an active part in the survival of Native traditions by helping tribal peoples comprehend the inescapable pressures of a modern, white-dominated world. He remained true to that task all his life, no matter what course it took. As an anthropologist, he called for the scientific (i.e., objective and unbiased) handling of Native materials. And as a writer of fiction and poetry, his purpose was no different, nor less effective. He wanted to write about the life he knew in Montana but, as he wrote John Collier early in 1934 when he applied for a job on the Commission, not in the "romantic vein in which it has been dealt with in the past."[12] His novels may be viewed as bridges between Indian and Euramerican cultures with the intent that, once read, they would lead to a subtle yet crucial change of perception on the part of his readers.

His was a monumental undertaking, for to address the popular stereotypes of Native peoples he chose to challenge them in the very forum in which they were perpetuated: written fiction. He attempted to supplant romantic misconceptions with reality by helping the public see that Indians are not museum pieces, nor merely remnants of once powerful, "primitive" cultures who succumbed to the irresistible force of progress in the form of transplanted European culture, a "flood" of a new kind. The means by which he was able to accomplish this task were innovative and ancient, unique and ubiquitous. Bridges take a long time to build, and McNickle's were exceptionally difficult for they were meant to span a vast gulf. He persevered and was successful through his faith and wit.

McNickle must have begun writing his first novel, *The Surrounded*, as early as 1927. At the same time he was engaged in this long project, he also wrote a number of short stories and some poetry, including a long narrative poem entitled "The Third Daughter," which is also set in Montana.[13] Most of this creative spurt took place in New York, including some of the revision of the novel he was attempting to publish. They were trying, frustrating times for the young author. Every publisher he contacted expressed an interest in his novel, originally entitled "The Hungry Generations." Negotiations were often very warm at first, but they would cool and he would find himself back where he started, with a manuscript. But there was encouragement also. In a copy of a letter written by Charles Pearce, the editor for Harcourt and Brace broke with tradition and quoted from the confidential reports of his readers, one of whom thought the manuscript might be "the beginning of a new Indian literature to rival that of Harlem."[14]

In retrospect, one recognizes how insightful this reader was, but, despite such praise, McNickle's book remained unpublished and he was forced to take menial jobs. Although they allowed him to survive, they took time and energy away from his efforts to write fiction; they took him away from the path he had chosen years before when he continued his schooling. Married, with a child on the way, his life was not the one he had hoped for with the sale of his allotment on the Flathead Reservation. The continual rejection by publishers wore heavily on a sensitive ego—but also quite possibly led to his ultimate success, as his diaries of those years reveal.

In Grenoble, France, in 1931, on a lonely night walk after an "embarrassing incident" at dinner which he does not record, he gives a brief glimpse of his insecurity as a social animal in Euramerican culture. Evidently, his acquaintances engaged him in conversation and, although he felt confident in his own intellectual ability, he was unable to express himself clearly. "I cannot find a single word to utter—or if I do I stutter."[15] He seeks what he calls "maturity": the ability to communicate his ideas to an audience effectively, confidently.[16]

Two days later, McNickle notes his elation at the revision of a passage of his novel in which Archilde, the protagonist, comes "down from the hill, filled with the emotion, the experience of which poetry is made."[17] These two diary entries—and other early entries—highlight his sense of inadequacy when required to engage spontaneously in conversation, but as a writer he revels in the power of his voice. Written narrative allowed McNickle to express his feelings and ideas in ways that he could not when called upon to do so spontaneously, orally. The writing of a novel allowed him time to reflect, deliberate, and revise, or, in other words, the time to bring to bear the subtle virtuosity of a storyteller as in Salish/Cree (Métis) verbal arts, where spontaneity is the result of long rehearsal. McNickle's novels demonstrate his ability to adopt, and adapt, a means of expression that was in many ways foreign to his family's experience, as well as his own childhood.

However, his novel was continually rejected by publishers. It lacked something. He had not yet realized the strategies he needed to make his novel appealing to a general audience yet remain true to the cultural material, the world view, he wished to explore. He arrived at this realization eventually, and the way that he came to it says a great deal about the endurance of his early education with his family, and in school.

The motivations behind his long search for a successful writing style are easy to understand. Since the objective of the mission and Indian boarding school systems of McNickle's day was to foster the assimilation of Indian peoples through the re-education of their children, instruction often meant instilling in them the motivation to change; they were tantalized with the American Dream, the epitome of "American values, culture, and aspirations." Once aware of the potential for material prosperity in American society, the logic went, Indian children could not help but want to become a part of it through study and personal industry. As the Commissioner of Indian Affairs wrote of the schools' purpose in 1901: "Dissatisfaction with their [Indian students'] present condition is inculcated that it may instill the desire to emulate the white man in his higher civilization."[18] The possibility for their complete integration, for their full acceptance by the wardens of this higher civilization, was never questioned, of course. But there is an "American Dream" that predates the one brought to this continent by the European; for the young McNickle, two conflicting concepts of the Dream intersected briefly during his years in school.

The idea that education may lead to material security can be found throughout Salish, Cree, and other Native literatures. Their stories tell of victories of heroic individuals who triumph over adversity through the acquisition of knowledge—and therefore power.

This generalization, of course, could apply universally. F. Scott Fitzgerald's Jay Gatsby defines greatness in terms of influence and therefore power, and both Hemingway's heroes and Faulkner's villains seek a similar power of self-determination. For the characters in Native verbal arts, however, triumphs invariably are defined by their benefit for the community, rather than simply the material prosperity of the individuals themselves. The stories emphasize the primal American Dream of communality, rather than the individuality so central to American literature since colonial times. The spoken stories also record the origins of ceremonies and rituals, the birth of places of power, the use of personal power on behalf of one's people, and so on, while dramatizing the ways that one may gain knowledge. Universally, they work to the benefit of the culture to which they belong. And McNickle remembered the stories. As the efforts of his lifetime reflect, the impetus behind the communal dream remained strong as he worked to achieve a degree of personal success as well.

To fulfill both dreams, McNickle had to accomplish two things: learn more about his intended audience and develop a means of expression suited to it. He knew that his knowledge of Euramerican culture was insufficient for his task, as was his ability to express his ideas forcefully, and so he began a course of study that would teach him how to revise his novel to make it both marketable and adequate to his purpose. To develop a clearer understanding of his readers, he delved systematically and wholeheartedly into their culture. His search was arduous, but his motivation was strong and in keeping with an attitude he acquired as a child: anything is possible if one has the knowledge necessary. His mother hoped education would allow him to direct his own future; thus, in this simple maxim, the two educational systems of his youth intersected.

The Salish and Cree have a great regard for education, but education unlike the one McNickle experienced at the mission school, Chemawa, and the university. For Native peoples in general, knowledge may be derived directly from one's world in a number of ways (all of which will be discussed in length in connection with *The Surrounded*). Two of these—the vision quest and verbal arts—are crucial to an understanding of the course of McNickle's education. There is no evidence to suggest that he had participated directly in visionary experiences while growing up in Montana, yet his search for knowledge, perhaps ironically, has the form of a traditional quest. McNickle went alone and with few provisions into the surrounding land to gain power. Salish and Cree literatures record such events, and the stories themselves are another way to knowledge. It was in them that McNickle found a successful voice as a storyteller and as a novelist. When he wrestled with the obstacles to his success as an author, alone and isolated from his family and his people, he tapped two resources: a tribal analysis of event, both literary and personal, and a wealth of Euramerican written literature.

At the university, where McNickle majored in English literature, he became aware of the potential of the written word, through which a vast body of information may be gained. Throughout his life, he went to the writings of those people whose thoughts, opinions, and theories formed social debate and therefore the society he wished to understand and influence. His diaries from the 1920s and 1930s provide valuable, early insights into this development of his character and habits: "At twenty-six I have very poor equipment for writing—for I do agree with him [Stuart P. Sherman] that a writer must combine many arts and have in him much of the scholar. But in the past few years I have not been improvident with my time and I know that I shan't in future."[19] And in a later entry, McNickle describes his idea of the creative process: "Inspiration gives the plan, and it should give much of the details of a piece of writing—but it is wearisome, intolerable labor that binds the whole together."[20] These, perhaps better than any other passages, give a summary of his approach and also his strength as a writer. His Salish/Cree background provided the inspiration, but these Native "details" found form only through careful craftmanship and scholarly research. Other passages from the same diary, as well as from later diaries, record his insights into and interpretations of a number of books that cover the broad spectrum of Western experience: history, literature, biology, political science. His reading list is indeed impressive; he mentions Stuart P. Sherman's *Americans* immediately before an allusion to Dostoyevsky's *The Idiot*. Two years later, still hard at work, he mentions *The Education of Henry Adams* and notes what may be his perception of his own history: "A boy's will is his life, and he dies when it is broken, as the colt dies in harness, taking a new nature in becoming tamed."[21]

McNickle's own "new nature" evolved during the years he spent revising his book's manuscript, but it emerged from more than his study of Western literature; he went to plays, lectures, and even a class on the writing of poetry taught by Robert Frost. There were also baseball games when Babe Ruth played for the Yankees, blissful nights at home listening to a seemingly endless series of classical productions on his first radio, and trips to museums and art galleries. This was the "good life" that his school teachers had no doubt told him about, and by living it he gained, quite literally, knowledge of the culture to which he was to address his writings. It took several years in the mainstream before he was able to reach his audience.

However, his diaries reveal two distinct aspects of his character. They contain long, descriptive passages that capture his sense of his surroundings. One describes a late summer thunderstorm, and then McNickle's astonishment at the sun's rapid southerly movement with the season, a movement he seems not to have noticed for a few days. He notes that the sun no longer sets at the end of his street, and then remembers that the Wednesday before was the last evening that it had.[22] McNickle is at one moment the dedicated student of American culture as he consciously and deliberately gathers knowledge about his world from its books. At another he is a young Métis man from Montana deriving insights directly from his experience and finding ample subjects for comment in the world's—and society's—movements and changes. Ironically, his vision quest took him through a world of libraries and museums and ballparks, as well as storms and seasons of the sun, and he drew on all resources to achieve his goal.

Both of these aspects of his character helped him revise and sell his book: one part inspiration and one part wearisome labor; one part Métis and one part Anglo. His resolution of the two perspectives led to an innovative approach to written narrative more representative of current Native fiction than the works that preceded it, and the story of how he discovered it is quite interesting. Through a series of fortuitous events, by 1935 he had struck upon the format that would explore the core of Native cultures that he saw persisting in this modern world of airplanes, long-distance communication, and global concerns—a core that remains intact today, partly as a result of McNickle's efforts.

"The Hungry Generations"

> Thou wast not born for death, immortal Bird!
>> No hungry generations tread thee down;
> The voice I hear this passing night was heard
>> In ancient days by emperor and clown:
> Perhaps the self-same song that found a path
>> Through the sad heart of Ruth, when, sick for home,
>> She stood in tears amid the alien corn;
>>> The same that oft-times hath
> Charm'd magic casements, opening on the foam
>> Of perilous seas, in fancy lands forlorn.
>
> *(John Keats, "Ode to a Nightingale")*

The one early draft of *The Surrounded* remaining in McNickle's papers at the Newberry is handwritten and three hundred and thirty-nine pages long. When compared with the final draft, it differs considerably, and the changes he made provide valuable insights into the development of McNickle's vision and his creative capabilities. Even the simplest of revisions speaks of a major change in the perception of its author.

Unlike all three of his published novels, this initial attempt at writing a long narrative does not open *in medias res*. Although he was aware of the technique—the Latin term is noted in a diary dating from 1930—McNickle was not yet aware of this simple device's potential; he had not yet recognized its pervasive use in Native verbal arts, nor the implications such use carries. For a Native audience, an *in medias res* opening suggests continuity from the past to the present by implying that the actions depicted are connected to others that preceded them. It ties one brief narrative into the longer, endless narrative of a people, because it evokes a shared history, a shared literary canon in which numerous stories and episodes share similar motifs. In brief, it is an unstated allusion which provides a literary/social context through which the current actions may be assessed, or judged. Its omission in the draft suggests that early in the composition process, as McNickle searched for his creative voice, he had not yet recognized how the stories he heard as a child related to his own life as an artist, nor how their basic motifs might enliven the revision of the novel he wrote while living in another culture with its own set of conventional narrative devices, devices he seemed incapable of mastering in any exceptional way.

The manuscript opens with an exposition of Archilde's recent past in Portland, Oregon. However, once the explication is complete and the action begins, the descriptive strength, the Salish/Métis inspiration of McNickle's diaries and later published works, emerges. One long paragraph that has a counterpart in the final draft describes in minute detail the landscape that Archilde and his mother scan as they sit silently letting the joy of his arrival home have its effect. Horses graze lazily in a pasture below the house, and Archilde notes how the flies bother them. He sees the mountains just a short distance away, and the stream he fished as a young boy: "Archilde's eyes wandered from one sight to another; everything was as familiar and natural as the air he breathed."[23]

The careful description continues throughout, and it provides a great deal of the narrative power for the manuscript. Likewise, McNickle uses many verbal phrasings and sayings quite early in the draft that seem to give a strong sense of place and social custom. When his mother first sees him, she acknowledges his arrival with humor: "So you have come back. . . . You don't look fat" (1). And when he meets later with his sister, Agnes, she says, "An Indian knows his home," which McNickle crossed out and replaced with, "A wolf knows his hole" (13). There are, therefore, very conscious attempts to employ aspects of Salish culture and voice in this early draft—ample evidence of his sense of place and people and lifeway. However, there are also very conscious efforts to package these cultural cues in a narrative conspicuously attuned to current literary trends. Despite the manuscript's inspired use of an autobiographical landscape and tribal mannerisms, its plot is not concerned with the detailed exploration of Salish culture and perception that one finds in *The Surrounded*.

The manuscript contains a section—over one hundred and twenty-five pages in length—of Archilde's experiences in Paris. This was written in the late twenties and early thirties, and thus has an autobiographical foundation in McNickle's visit to France then, but the reasons that McNickle felt compelled to devote a major portion of his novel to the Paris of that era also derive from another impetus. He was writing for a white audience; therefore, he wrote of things in literary vogue. Drawing upon his own experiences, he created Parisian settings and characters that would be familiar to readers lured to expatriate literature, from James to Joyce to Fitzgerald. He gives us Hemingway's capital of Western literature and art in transition, the mecca for writers and artists from all over the globe. He carefully notes specific places in Paris, draws the local color of café and inexpensive hotel, and, like Hemingway, has his main character move freely and confidently in a foreign land, fully accepted by the locals. In fact, the early title of the book—"The Hungry Generations"—suggests Gertrude Stein's term for the American expatriates in Paris: "The Lost Generation." It also summarizes McNickle's feelings about this influential generation of European and American intellectuals, feelings that he expressed quite strongly in the manuscript and which ran counter to the images of the vibrant, dynamic lifestyles of Hemingway, Fitzgerald, Anderson, and other literary figures.

In Paris, Archilde's first friendship develops with a young American pianist named Feure, who is preparing for a concert tour of Europe. Through him, Archilde meets Claudia, the daughter of a man who made his fortune in the railroads that opened the American West for exploitation by Europeans and who, in turn, has been railroaded into an urbane, sedentary, pointless life in Europe by his shrewish wife. (In fact, this may be McNickle's idea of poetic justice for those who exploited the West: hell for a man of action and adventure.) Claudia takes Archilde's training as a social animal in hand and guides him through the inner circles of the city's intellectual set, where he makes quite an impression. Unlike McNickle, Archilde does not falter. When called upon to voice an opinion, he responds frankly and readily: "He had a knack of speaking in simple, plain phrases that brought his story before his listeners with the greatest clearness. He was not aware of it and would have doubted anyone who called his attention to it."[24]

Like McNickle, Archilde possesses a highly developed power of observation, and what he sees in "the good life" is not what he expected. He discovers that Feure is a homosexual, which does not bother him as much as the realization that the man will forever prepare for, but never make, his concert tour of Europe. Like the rest of the expatriates, Feure wants "to live easily and at the cost of no effort" and perhaps consume himself in doing so, as his name suggests (210). The men of Paris are unhealthy and ineffectual because they do not want to *do* anything. Ironically, these questers after knowledge and truth are static and, worse yet, complacent. They inhabit a world of abstraction in which they need never change, endlessly engaged in debate without purpose or application. They seek but will never translate findings into actions, and therefore they will never benefit their people. In McNickle's view, this lifeway was a dead end, and the lives of the people who lived it were hollow and insignificant. As in Keats's ode, Paris is, indeed, a "fancy land forlorn." Archilde returns home.

The title of the manuscript is an obvious allusion to Keats's and Stein's term, but it is also an apt description of the Salish and Métis people on reservations in the 1930s who, like McNickle's own family, hungered for the power to direct their own lives and futures. This power had been taken from them by the steady encroachment of white immigrants and governmental officials, and as McNickle's mother learned, it is extremely difficult, if not impossible, to recover. McNickle's purpose in this early draft was to find some mediary point, some balance between two cultures that often battle for control over lives and land. Perhaps the writing of Archilde's story was also his way of working out his own peace between his two backgrounds and his education in two distinct, sometimes contradictory perceptions of the world. "The Hungry Generations" certainly presents a clear resolution to the dilemma Archilde faces from his mixed heritage. He inherits his father's ranch and the manuscript ends with him financially secure and content with his lot, the Indian assimilated and happy at last.[25]

At this point in McNickle's development, he wanted to feed the hungry generations on individuality and materialism, not on the values that traditionally have sustained Native cultures on this continent. The manuscript conforms to, and reinforces, popular perceptions of social progress by affirming contemporary American attitudes and ideals: Archilde achieves the American Dream.

In short, the manuscript is closely aligned with trends in other American novels current to its writing, including the popular novels written *about* Indians by Anglos. In fact, one such work, *Laughing Boy* by Oliver La Farge, won the Pulitzer prize in 1930, while McNickle was at work on his own novel. Despite La Farge's obvious attempt to portray Native people sympathetically, his characters are Anglos painted red, betrayed through their actions. Their motions provide an objective, withdrawn dissertation on Navajo culture: anthropological artifacts, fit for wonder and comparison, rather than insightful depictions of the process of being Navajo. As Leslie Marmon Silko and her Navajo students pointed out long ago, "as an expression of anything Navajo, especially with relation to Navajo emotions and behavior, the novel was a failure."[26] Despite his use of ceremonial gatherings and descriptive detail, La Farge and his readers remained removed from the intricate nature of Navajo lifeways and perceptions, which include an unspoken awareness of social relationships, a close tie to a specific landscape, an extensive knowledge of a shared history conveyed through verbal arts in which characters' actions bespeak their natures. *Laughing Boy*—its characters and story—came from Euramerican literatures, which heavily emphasize the cerebral machinations of characters in order to forward plot. And it was popular. It is also a fit example of the romantic ways in which many nontribal authors presented Native peoples, ways that McNickle wanted to avoid.

Yet, in his need to reach the same readers, he made concessions. Although in the manuscript Archilde possesses many traits that McNickle recognized in the Salish, and perhaps himself, such as a strong will, an undefined attraction to the land of his birth, and a confidence in his own ability, these qualities are eclipsed by his desire to be a part of the white world. His pilgrimage is to Paris, not into the Mission Mountains like his predecessors in tribal verbal arts. By the end of the book he is granted his wish when he becomes a prominent member of white society. Needless to say, the manuscript does not contain the powerful Salish characters found in the finished product. His mother's character is not fully developed; she plays only a minor and brief role in the plot. The powerful uncle Modeste, who tells stories of the past, is not to be found. Their absence is understandable because at this point McNickle, like La

Farge, was concerned with an individual, Archilde, not with a character whose actions reflect a people's beliefs and perceptions and durability as a culture.

The major Salish events that form the central plot of *The Surrounded* are not to be found either, because McNickle had not yet realized how durable Native cultures are. In fact, they came as the result, ironically, of McNickle's involvement with other Native peoples and cultures as a governmental agent, and, even earlier, as a biographer of a scholar who studied ancient oral texts. Thanks to these jobs, McNickle began to see the histories and the contemporary conditions of American Indians in a broader context than his own incomplete, personal knowledge allowed, and the form and substance of his novel changed radically. It was transformed from an exhortation on American ideals to the affirmation of Salish. The core of cultural integrity that persists and is exemplified by participation in ceremonies, the survival of ancient social patterns and governments, and the oral literature that transmits culture from one generation to the next were late inclusions. His vision was taking shape.

As early as the spring of 1934, McNickle began to explore the engaging power of Native narratives. At this time he lived in Tuckahoe, New York, and was employed by James T. White and Company, which was compiling the *National Cyclopaedia of American Biography*. In this capacity, he was directed to write a biography of Professor William Gates, who was on the faculty of Johns Hopkins University and recognized for his work with the ancient Native cultures of what are now called Mexico and Central America. Gates's work captured McNickle's imagination, so much so in fact that he wrote to him to ask for a job. He saw Gates as scrupulous in his examinations of Native cultures because his work was "scientific, that is to say exacting, unexhibitionary, and removed from the sentimental and inept efforts that have been made in behalf of the Indian in the past and which have succeeded only in making the uplifters ridiculous and sinking the victim into deeper obscurity."[27] The letter is a persuasive piece of writing, due largely to McNickle's obvious enthusiasm for the topic of Native stories. It also reveals a great deal about his own goals and desires at this point in his life.

McNickle wanted to join Gates in his work, but he admitted that he did not have the training needed. Instead, he offered what he considered to be its equivalents: a deep concern for Native peoples and a creative imagination. He notes his writings to date, including his one book, "a fictionalized study of the development of an Indian boy." Once his credentials as a writer of fiction have been proffered, he makes his proposal:

> Would it be possible, for instance, to compile a tentative history of the Maya people from information you have thus far uncovered? Are there any separate tales or episodes which might be exhumed and saved from a second burial in a Ph.D. thesis? I could not undertake to write learnedly in the field, but neither do I mean to vulgarize the material for Boy Scout publications and their kind. In brief, is there and [*sic*] material that might be dealt with creatively—made alive? Understand, I have my own resources as to material. I am not looking for a "field" to exploit. I have never taken a step for the sake of finding "local color" nor pried into one person's affairs for the sake of getting a "character." If writing does not emerge naturally from one's experiences it can serve no purpose except to engulf people more profoundly in the meaninglessness in which most of them live.[28]

Gates and he corresponded many more times, but McNickle was never offered a job. However, his desire to write a history ultimately found form in future works: in particular the anthropological/historical *They Came Here First* (1949) and his second novel, *Runner in the Sun: A Story of Indian Maize* (1954). For the present, as he says in the letter, he had his own material, and it was Salish.

At this point, the revision of the manuscript began moving in a new direction, toward a closer examination of Salish culture through the conscious use of verbal arts and oral narratives. Within three months, he would write to Marius Barbeau for permission to include a story published in his book *Indian Days in the Canadian Rockies*.[29] This story and others were written into the next draft of the book. Owing to his assignment as Gates's biographer, his reading list had expanded to include collections of stories from Native cultures, as well as the works from Euramerican culture that had occupied so much of his time and effort over the preceding four years. His dual backgrounds were once again complementing one another; his experiences as a university student and biographer helped him conduct research on oral narratives, the findings of which were in turn enlightened by his childhood experiences in an oral culture. He was beginning to build a repertoire and, like a traditional storyteller, to use his own creative imagination to fit the stories to the general audience he desired to reach with his novel—but without altering the basic values and attitudes they dramatize. And his purpose was clear: to make his own narrative come to life and thereby raise his audience from "the meaninglessness in which most of them live."

The Surrounded was published on February 14, 1936, but the final revisions of the manuscript and galleys took place in the autumn and winter of 1935. At this time, McNickle had accepted a job on the staff of John Collier, director of the Commission on Indian Affairs. The job changed his life, quite literally. It gave him the financial security he needed as head of a family and therefore relieved some of the pressure to publish that he had been under for so long. It also placed him squarely in the middle of governmental controversy over the management of Indian affairs. To do his job as a mediator, he needed to extend his knowledge of past Indian/government relations. He also needed to interact with tribal peoples from all over the country. Through his efforts, he gained knowledge, and where he expected to see complete dominance by white culture and the irretrievable loss of traditional Native power, he found secret endurance and survival. The speech to the Missouri Archaeological Society discussed earlier dates from this time, as do letters that convey the same awareness. There are others that tell of the direction his research took.

One is a reply (dated October 6, 1935) to a letter from Constance Skinner who had read a late manuscript of the novel and responded enthusiastically. He had not completed his revision of it, though, and he had decided "to get a study room at the Congressional library and spend my evenings there. Another month ought to result in a fresh start."[30] By this point, he had arrived at the structure and content of the published novel: Skinner mentions the Salish scope of the book as well as the sheriff, both of which allude to late additions to the text. The final adjustments took place when he had access to a wealth of printed ethnographic material.

This approach to fiction is a subtle yet radical shift in his role as a novelist. No longer was he the sole creative force behind his work—a novelist alone in his cold room seeking truth and understanding—but a storyteller searching for the right stories and style to convey his purpose. The distinction requires elaboration. McNickle's early draft emerged from his own experiences—his years in Montana and his time in Paris—and it followed the conventions of other contemporary American narratives. Although autobiographical in inspiration, it was to be read by his Anglo audience as fiction, as the imaginative creation of one individual's mind and as one individual's interpretation of his world. When McNickle included actual stories and ceremonies from Native canons and cultures, he moved the novel toward ethnography, toward a *cultural autobiography* that demonstrates traditional, Native ways of perceiving the world, perpetuating beliefs, and therefore ensuring their endurance as a culture. Although a fictional account, it remained true to those beliefs and ways. In short, McNickle's success in revising his novel came when he employed the strategies and motifs of the verbal arts. To make his contemporary story about Archilde understandable for an uninitiated audience, he first had to tell the stories of his people that relate directly to Archilde's. To make his audience understand that Native cultures are alive and vital, he had to create a story both to explain and to demonstrate the means for their endurance. And to engage his audience, largely Euramerican, he had to employ the conventions of narrrative it expected.

He extracted from written accounts types of stories he had heard firsthand as a child but possibly never understood because he was too young and too involved to be objective. In addition, he had no basis for comparison with another culture until he left home to go to school. Once he had compared and analyzed, however, he drew from the written canon both the novel genre and the ethnographic detail to incorporate in it, and the prepatory note to *The Surrounded* lists his sources. Like his mother before him, he learned to use the resources of his audience in his attempt to persuade and enlighten it, but he brought both written and verbal conventions to his narrative. He did not reproduce verbatim the renditions of stories and actions he found in the works of Barbeau, Fitzgerald, and the others. Instead, he revised them to resemble more closely the events of oral storytelling that he had experienced as a child.

This need for accuracy in rendering them to the printed page led McNickle to search for the absolutes of Native oral literatures, for irreducible qualities, attitudes, ideas, or concepts that remain unchanged even when stories are altered by storytellers or ethnographers. His exploration resulted in the structure of the central plot in *The Surrounded*: the story of Archilde's education, his "development" as McNickle called it in his letter to Gates. In order to appreciate fully this innovative blend of two uses of fictional narrative and the complexity the mixture adds to the novel itself, one must first explore the basic perceptions of the world conveyed through the object of McNickle's study—the Salish.

The Salish

Originally from far to the north and west, the Salish migrated long ago to the land they now inhabit. When they arrived, their stories tell us, they found a race of people they called the Foolish Folk, because their self-centered actions always placed these short, dark people in precarious situations. Rather than work as a people, the Foolish Folk moved individually, getting in each other's way and laughing at one another's misfortune.[31] These qualities seemed absurd to the Salish, and the extinction of these first inhabitants of their land emphasizes, in Salish literature, the desirability of a communal approach. A lesson was learned, and in the stories the Salish tell, beginning with one rendition of their creation, one finds a continuous emphasis on the acquisition of the knowledge of how to act responsibly in a world which makes survival a tenuous proposition:

> Before the world was created, a son was born to a very powerful woman, Skomeltem. The son's name is Amotken, which means "he who sits on top of the mountain," for his home is on the summit of the covering of the earth. Amotken created heaven and earth and mankind. He created other worlds also, worlds under and above and around us. His mother lives alone on one of those worlds beyond the waters.
>
> The first human beings that Amotken created became very

wicked and turned a deaf ear to his teachings and warnings. Angry with them, he drowned all of them in a great flood. Then he created a second tribe, twice as tall as the first. But they became even more wicked than the first people, and so Amotken destroyed them by fire from heaven. He created a third tribe; when they became as wicked as the first, he destroyed them by a pestilence. The fourth tribe would have been destroyed also had not Amotken's mother begged him to let them live. She so softened the anger of Amotken that he promised never to destroy his creations again.

Until the time of the fourth tribe, the world was in darkness, for there was no sun. Believing that the sole cause of their wickedness was the darkness, the people held a council to discuss the matter. These were the animal people—animals that could reason and talk. All of them refused to be the sun except Sinchlep, or Coyote. He was the smartest and most powerful of the animal people. But when Coyote was the sun and passed over the land, he saw what everyone was doing. And he called out, so that all might hear, even the secret doings of people. The evildoers angrily took Coyote by the tail, which at that time was very long, and brought him back to the ground. They told him that he could no longer be the sun.

Crow then offered to be the sun. But as he was really black all over, he gave very little light. People laughed at him. Unable to endure their ridicule, Crow gave up the task in shame.

Amotken, though invisible, had several sons, one of whom was Spokani. Seeing the people's need for light, he sent Spokani down to be the sun. Spokani, wishing to marry a woman from the earth, landed in a camp of Flatheads. People thought him very handsome but so different from themselves that they refused to admit him to their lodges.

Disappointed, Spokani left the place. Nearby, he saw a family of frogs to whom he complained about the treatment their neighbors had given him. One of the frogs, very large and fat, said that she was willing to marry him; she would be happy to become the wife of Amotken's son. With a jump she attached herself to one cheek of Spokani.

The neighboring people, seeing the disfigured cheek, were so angry that they tried to kill the frog with sticks. She remained on Spokani's cheek. She begged him to leave the earth and become the sun at once.

And so Spokani became the sun. To revenge himself for the contempt of the people, he does not allow them to see him closely during the day but covers himself with a shining robe. As night approaches, he removes his robe, crosses the waters under the earth, and then only shows himself as he is. Then he is the moon. The spots on the moon are the frog on his cheek.[32]

For someone raised in the traditions of the Judeo-Christian world, this story is indeed curious. For someone who works in the written traditions of Western culture, this story at first glance appears simplistic, almost childlike. That was, historically, the first response to Native oral stories by European colonists and scholars. However, McNickle—as well as modern literary scholars and anthropologists—began to view them not solely in terms of *what* the stories state but also in terms of how they state it. When he began to examine oral stories systematically, McNickle found that the actions that take place speak more directly to Native perceptions of the world than the characters themselves, who are bound by the limitations of temporality.

One immediately recognizable point of interest in the story above is that the creator is not the initial force in the universe nor the creation the initial act. Instead, one finds that he also was created, born of a powerful woman. In effect, the universe before the creation was not a void, nor is the creator (as an individual) the ultimate power in it. The universe was peopled by beings whose actions and powers may be understood and explained in terms of the lifeways practiced by the Salish themselves. The creation of the Salish, then, is presented as one event in an ancient, ongoing process that can be encompassed in narrative. In fact, we are told that today's race is the fourth attempt by Amotken. Obviously, he is not infallible; he makes mistakes and must correct them. Here, creation is not a plan, a rigid scheme brought into being at one point in time for all eternity, but a trial-and-error process that must be responsive to unforeseen or changing circumstances. The first three tribes refuse to learn and therefore to change, and their extinction is Amotken's response to their inflexibility. As the Salish say of the Foolish Folk, ignorance is wicked and the knowledge of how to act leads to survival: the creator found in this body of literature places a high

premium on education, on the ways to knowledge and self-suffi-
ciency.

The Salish are Amotken's fourth attempt at creating human beings. The number four—as in the four cardinal directions, the four
seasons, and so on—is sacred to many Native peoples and, as here,
it acts as a framework in many stories from their literatures. The
creation of humans is carried out in four steps, but the process also
contains the destruction of the first three tribes. One way of destruction, the great flood, can be found in many of the oral literatures of
this continent, and it has a worldwide distribution. Similarly, the
"fire from heaven" and pestilence seem to parallel Judeo-Christian
literature. Debates have raged over such bits of similarity, but the
important thing to recognize for this study is that the references may
have been the conscious attempt by the storyteller to relate his tale
to his audience, to the background of the ethnographer who collected this story. Their inclusion is ample evidence of one of oral
narrative's greatest strengths: its ability, through the efforts of the
storyteller, to accommodate changes in the world while maintaining its own, distinct character, including an inherent framework on
which the storyteller may improvise. And McNickle recognized
these innate qualities in verbal narrative events.

The creation is the first event noted; the second is the council of
the people. Here, the story moves into another mode of creation
and, simultaneously, another way to knowledge. No longer is
Amotken the force that works to transform the world. Instead, his
creations take the task in hand. The animal people gather to discuss
a problem and reason a solution. Through their own initiative, they
become unified by a common goal and course of action. Their
recognition of the need for light is an interesting leap in awareness,
for it posits a solution—the sun—that is beyond their current realm
of knowledge and experience but is reached through communal
reflection and communication. As a result of their unification, they
become an active force in their world and, again, a trial-and-error
process guides the course of action. Moreover, an individual is
called upon to act on behalf of the community, but an unfortunate
choice is made; Coyote is noted for his quickness to point out
human weaknesses. The decision to transform the world does not
guarantee a smooth and orderly transition; great care must be taken

to monitor the process and adapt to changing conditions. Coyote, the source of the people's embarrassment, is removed. The next candidate, however, sheds too little light—as opposed to Coyote's too much light—and the need for a beneficial balance between the two remains.

Creation is an ongoing process of dealing with fluctuating influences in the world, and it transcends the individual. Even Amotken is created and is moved by the forces of need and knowledge. Once his people have begun to learn for themselves, they share in his own power, and he attempts to aid them. However, his son is first shunned because he is different and then attacked because of the frog on his cheek. The people once again demonstrate their ignorance. They respond inappropriately, twice, to two extreme views of personal, outward appearance. They attack what they see as a disfigurement on a being they refused to entertain because he is too beautiful, too perfect. As a result of their actions, they lose part of the power Spokani brought to them. He brings light to all beings, including the Salish, but he cloaks himself from the people half the time. Another valuable lesson is conveyed through the narrative: the world is plastic; it can be molded by certain powers. Amotken has this power, but the people can also transform the world, through knowledge or through ignorance. The story of the creation demonstrates both possibilities, and thus the need for moderation, for balance.

But other forces are at work in the world. Sometimes evil thwarts the actions of the people, and the stories demonstrate the ways to balance the effects of evil. In the tales of Sinchlep—some sources call him Coyote—one finds that the materials needed to overcome the ill effects of evil are ever present; all one needs is the knowledge of how to employ them.

Coyote is a well known character in many Native oral literatures. He is a trickster/culture-hero who possesses peculiarly human foibles. Likewise, in many traditions when Coyote acts he does so out of self-interest, often in an attempt to fulfill his own desires and needs at the expense of other people. One story that has a wide distribution on this continent tells of his devious plan to marry his own daughters. His human, carnal desires are the focus of the storyteller's scorn and humor; usually Coyote's actions bring him pain and anguish, but quite often they become somehow beneficial for the community at large through the lessons they teach.

These lessons are found in Salish literatures, but the Foolish Folk provide them; thus, in their tradition, Coyote/Sinchlep is quite often a culture-hero, a major benefactor of the people. One story even makes him the motive force behind the creation of humankind. In this way, his individual character is de-emphasized, since flawed traits are not the focus of the narrative. Instead, his actions become prominent because they encapsulate the knowledge and ways to knowledge heroes employ; the ways that he moves hold the qualities with which the storyteller is concered. One such story is recorded by Clark (1966), which I will paraphrase here in its significant elements. (See Appendix, "Creation of the Red and White Races.")

After the world and the animal people are created, Coyote grows lonely, so he goes to Old Man in the Sky—referred to afterwards simply as Old Man—and asks him for a people of his own. He needs someone to talk with and care for, and Old Man, tired of Coyote's constant visits and wailing, agrees. However, the job of collecting the materials Old Man needs for the creative act falls to Coyote. He must go to a specific place in the land where the correct soil is to be found. The weight of action once again falls to the individual, and to fulfill his need he must make a journey to gain, from the environment, the basic element of human existence.

After he fills his bag with the red soil, however, he is overcome with fatigue. It has been a long journey, and he must rest for his return. As he sleeps, his perennial enemy, Mountain Sheep, plays a trick on him; he fills the bottom half of the bag with white dirt. When Coyote returns to Old Man, the sun has set and so both of them fail to notice the difference in the soils. Once again, Old Man is not infallible; he is limited, like humankind, by forces in the world, such as darkness. As a result of circumstance and Mountain Sheep's influence, two races are born when Coyote breathes life into the forms shaped by Old Man. Because Coyote recognizes that the two races will have difficulty living together, he orders the world by taking the white race to another land.

There are a number of similarities between the two creation stories, despite the vast differences in their overall "plots," their sequences of events. But the most obvious difference is the most interesting. In the latter story, one witnesses the birth of two races. No longer are Native Americans the sole inhabitants of this world; they must share it with white people. A change has come about in the land of the Salish, and their oral literature has acknowledged that change within its traditional framework and with its characteristic implications. The names of the characters are the same; they perform their usual activities; and the results are the same. The Salish are created and placed in their land. Amotken is still with them, and Coyote still protects them. He leaves the white race to its own devices and concentrates his efforts on the Salish, for whom he cares a great deal, as can be seen in other stories in which he acts to assure their survival.

In the story above, Coyote asks for a people to talk to and care for, and language is central to his concern and his influence. In other stories, he is appointed by Amotken to travel through the world and counter the influence of Amteep, the primal evil character. (See Appendix, "Amotken and Coyote.") When the latter uses his power to blight the staples of the Salish diet—berries, fruits, and vegetables—the established order of the world is disrupted and survival threatened. A crucial time is at hand, a time of change, and action is required to meet this new influence: "So Coyote persuaded the salmon and the trout to seek places of spawning in the freshwater streams, and he taught the Indians how to catch and prepare the fish for food."[33] When Amteep unleashes disease, Coyote transplants medicinal plants and teaches the people their use. When Amteep brings winter to the land, Coyote teaches the people to make clothing and shelters.

The way to survival is established. Evil can transform the world, but the people can affect their world also. The means to do so exist in the landscape; the potentiality is there. They need only the knowledge—an education in the correct actions, the things they must do—to tap the potential and benefit from it. Sinchlep/Coyote is the primal educator in this way. But what is the basis of his power? Another story will illustrate.

There are a number of curious things to note in the story of "The Ram's Horn Tree." (See Appendix.) For one thing, it begins *in medias res*, just as do the other stories examined here. Coyote has been traveling a long time, and, like all travelers, he is weary. At such times, he is likely to make mistakes. He steps on Meadow Lark, the messenger, who has come to warn him of danger. Coyote corrects his error by using his power to set the broken leg and speed its healing, and Meadow Lark then warns him of an evil mountain sheep who inhabits a mountain pass that is on Coyote's route. Rather than change course and travel in a different direction, Coyote deliberates—and then decides. Amotken has given him the task of confronting evil beings, and sometimes these take the shape of unforeseen obstacles to movement or restrictions to freedom of choice. Coyote will stay on his path and face the danger because Amotken has also promised him the power to remove barriers that would otherwise rule his freedom, but the evocation of this power requires certain actions on his part. Recognizing the potential for danger, he prepares himself accordingly. He sings his "power song and through his powers he got a magic flint knife."[34] Through his faith and his adherence to prescribed action—the motions by which one may prepare to confront evil—Coyote gains a tool necessary to destroy the ram. His arsenal is not complete, however.

Wickedness and evil are related to ignorance; to counter their influence, one needs both the ability to recognize them and the knowledge of how to react. When confronted by the ram, "Coyote began to get a little worried." He wonders if his power will be stronger than his adversary's and if the correct course of action will come to him when necessary. Coyote recognizes his own fallibility and the ever-changing nature of the world; one can never be sure. To silence his doubt, he begins to question his foe. He goes to his adversary to gain the necessary knowledge. He finds that the ram intends to fight him because, simply, it is his turn; the ram fights everyone who travels through the pass. The illogic of his reasoning betrays the ram's inherent inflexibility, his weakness—his arrogant pride in his own strength and refusal to alter his actions to accommodate changing conditions. There is no doubt here, only stupidity. Through his patient wit, Coyote gains another weapon. He uses the ram's arrogance against him by challenging him to prove his power. When the ram strikes a nearby tree to show off, his horns are embedded and he is at the mercy of Coyote, who easily beheads him with the flint knife. The horns remain in the tree to mark a place of power where an individual triumphed over evil through faith and reason. Here, people's wishes may be realized, even today, if they take the correct actions.

Reflection reveals some similarities in the four stories. In each, someone is confronted with the need to respond to an undesirable element in the world: the darkness that nurtures wickedness, Coyote's loneliness, Amteep's evil influence, and the mountain sheep. In each, the possibility to work a transformation in the world is taken for granted; the only question is *how* to remove the unwanted influence. This knowledge is defined as power, and knowledge may be gained in several ways, through a number of actions. In the first instance, communal action is employed; the council reasons and discusses its way to a process that will reap the desired result. In the second, a personal quest or journey provides the thing desired by the individual but also results in the creation of the people. In the third and fourth, the power is given to Coyote by Amotken, and, in turn, it is passed along to the people by Coyote's travels through the land. In the latter story, one is shown how an individual taps his personal potential: the song concentrates his mental and physical movements on an articulation and celebration of his faith. He is rewarded with the flint knife. As in many Native contexts, movement and language are coincidental, and McNickle uses this idea to forge the powerful events in *The Surrounded*. In such events, the people receive the benefit—power and freedom of movement—through the hero's actions. In all the stories, whether a communal or a personal action is performed, the good of the people is both the desired goal and final result.

Unlike an audience, the characters in the stories do not have access to an oral tradition that charts past events: needs and the actions that fulfilled them. However, any participant well versed in the oral literature of the Salish possesses this information. He or she knows the stories that tell of changes that have taken place, that describe the actions taken to address these changes, and that mark places in the land where, and the ways that, power may be gained. If the contemporary Salish find their knowledge inadequate for present circumstances, the ways to gain added knowledge are apparent in the stories also. New stories may emerge, or old ones may be altered accordingly, to record the contemporary actions of individuals or the people at large. The stories above may imaginatively present primal events, but these become alive in the present world through the actions and attentiveness of real people. They may be told and thereby shared by a group of people, or they may be remembered by an individual confronting something in his or her life—a similar situation, a place where a story took place, or a person whose actions remind one of a being in a story—which calls forth the story. Associations between one's life story and a people's life story, which give meaning and animation to the Native world, are often at work upon McNickle, even when his accomplishments seem to mark his complete integration into white society. These general axioms of verbal cultures were a part of his character, and through them he found his power as a modern-day storyteller.

Although the stories above are from a collection compiled from various ethnographies and published in 1966, they focus on events that supposedly took place at the very beginning of humankind. Of course, one realizes that they are but an echo of a moment in time when human perceptions and language came together. Some may have originated in ancient times, others might be quite recent creations, and all have been touched by numerous storytellers, at least two ethnographers, and a few editors as well. The stories, like the tenuous existence and world they tell of, are mutable, yet in them McNickle recognized some very basic attitudes and concepts that do not change with shifting influences in the world, even sweeping changes such as European colonization: the process for solving problems and addressing threats to survival, the ways that knowledge may be acquired, the recognition that the world is plastic and that people may transform it through ignorance or through knowledge, the acceptance of humankind's fallibility, the need for reasonable flexibility. These are the absolutes that he found at work, the ancient values and understanding moving in modern times to maintain the cultural cores he saw surviving secretly against seemingly devastating odds. More importantly, for this study at least, McNickle found them through his study of published ethnographies, his memories of his childhood, and the conscious quest for knowledge that directed the former and clarified the latter. His study altered forever his perception of Native cultures. Quite literally, it resulted in a new vision. With the stories, he revised "The Hungry Generations" to change its voice from that of an American novelist writing about Indians to that of a storyteller employing a new form of "telling" to reach a new audience. The distinction becomes apparent in a close comparative analysis of the first draft and the published novel.

2   The Vision

The Surrounded

The publishers who read "The Hungry Generations" and later drafts
of his book praised McNickle's potential as a novelist. He was doing
something right, but he was not doing everything right. They would
not publish the manuscript even though, interestingly enough, the
early drafts presented Archilde in terms of society's ideal of assimilation. He was acceptable, at least in theory, to those who did not want
to recognize the systematic oppression of American Indians, explore
the reasons for it, or change it. Indeed, he is the Indian convert who
becomes a productive member of society—productive being a relative term, obviously. By becoming a successful, influential rancher,
the embryonic Archilde turns his life into a reinforcement of American values and ideals, including the American Dream. Ironically,
despite McNickle's talent, his manuscript offered nothing new,
nothing unique, because it echoed the conventions and perceptions
of the time. Seemingly, La Farge had written the better "Indian"
novel.

The Archilde one finds in the early handwritten manuscript is
moved only marginally by his heritage. There are very few scenes
that have a Salish tone, and these are undeveloped with one excep-
tion. The mysterious appearance of a song Archilde sings as he rides
his full hay wagon at book's end is one example of the ways in
which McNickle introduces a tidbit of tribal material:

> Then, of a sudden, certain words came into his mind, words such
> as he had never used before. One by one they pressed into his
> brain, each one bursting into a shower of light as when rockets end
> their flight and expire in bright flame. Each word had the breath of
> fire but it had, also the strength of cold metal.[1]

Archilde sings the song, against his will, and in so doing, acts as his people act; against his will, his people's history and culture and language take possession of him, and McNickle describes that possession in terms of light, sparks, and fire.

This is the final scene of the manuscript, its ultimate glimpse into McNickle's perception of contemporary Salish life. Given its placement and lack of development, it is inconsequential in the context of the whole work. Interestingly, the brevity and intensity of its description and the fact that it comes at the end of a long manuscript may suggest an autobiographical connection. The forces of culture and heritage that are at work on Archilde were also at work on McNickle as he wrote and revised his novel; language and articulation helped him question, and ultimately clarify. Archilde's song *is* inspirational, and McNickle relied upon inspiration. However, at the early date of the handwritten manuscript, his understanding of tribal perceptions was understandably limited. It took the painstaking labor of research before he could move beyond it. Midway through the manuscript there is another event that reveals even more about McNickle's view at this early stage of composition, and its details speak of the dramatic change that came over him when he began his final revisions.

The manuscript contains the seed of one of the plots found in *The Surrounded*. In both, Archilde witnesses the murder of the game warden in the mountains and covers up the deed to protect his mother. In the manuscript, he returns from Paris after she dies and his involvement is made public. He is arrested and put into jail, where he is coldly received by his fellow inmates while he awaits trial. They demand money, and, when he refuses, he is ostracized, left without food, attacked, and then hauled before a kangaroo court where he is found guilty for his failure to share with his comrades. The punishment is set. Archilde is given an icy bath and left alone in his cell to fend for himself. It is winter, and the cold has its effect. He becomes ill, develops a fever, and begins to hallucinate, at least that is one way to account for the dreams he has. If one knows a little about Salish, Cree, or Native cultures in general, another implication is possible.

Although carefully concealed, Archilde's ordeal is a variation of a traditional vision quest. As in the tradition, he fasts, he takes a cleansing bath that makes him sweat, and he is then left isolated until he has the vision he needs. But it is not a very pretty vision that McNickle describes:

> He stood arm in arm with his mother [who is dead] those days, breathing the unhealthy mist of a hundred generations before his day. Inhabitants of a bleak world into which the sunlight had not yet penetrated, these were his people. . . . When opposition and adversity overtook them and threatened death and starvation on the snowy flats of winter, they sat in a huddle before a sick fire and with blank eyes, awaited the hand to fall. They fought when the hand of the spirit pushed them forward—when it turned against them, they bowed their heads before the wind of wrath. Dull, naked, savage, the breath in their nostrils was fatalism—these were the hundred generations who stood behind Archilde.[2]

This is hardly a vision that a traditional vision seeker would find; it reflects, instead, what McNickle thought was an objective, scientific view of his ancestors, at least at this point in his development. As he wrote to William Gates, he wanted to avoid the highly romanticized, and therefore counterproductive, approach to Native materials that he saw in the works of others. Rather than idealize tribal peoples, he wanted to present them as he believed they must have been. Unfortunately, there was another possibility that he had not considered.

By trying to force objectivity, McNickle lost the substance of tribal cultures in an image that evokes the stereotypes of "primitive man" basic to the theory of Social Darwinism. Although "the spirit pushed them *forward*," the "savages" resisted (*emphasis added*). This is not an accurate image. In short, he went to the other extreme and fell victim to yet another form of excess which uses a Western set of criteria to judge a people's outward material condition and then applies that judgment to their inner being; their inactivity becomes a sign of ignorance, or stubbornness, or both. This betrays an ethnocentric view of other cultures, one that fails to consider nonmaterial aspects of their experience, in particular their beliefs, customs, ceremonial life, ideas of appropriate action, and literatures that convey all these things from one generation to the next. He was to change this view quite drastically.

The entire manuscript is shaded by the dark theme of fatalism expressed in Archilde's dream, and it is a trait that McNickle saw, then, as characteristic of tribal peoples. Archilde is moved continually by forces beyond his control. He is forced on a vision quest that takes him to his people's land of the dead. The old song comes to his lips without his permission, and he sings despite his desire to adopt Euramerican ways. As McNickle says, "a force was working that he [Archilde] did not recognize."[3] His will seems powerless, and he seems destined to become a blend of white and red cultures, not necessarily to the improvement of either, if the individualistic and materialistic nature of his success is considered. His future is sealed and unavoidable; he is fated for success, and the book ends with his enjoying his good fortune. Ironically, this happy ending is much more pessimistic than the bleak ending of *The Surrounded*, for fatalism disavows the freedom of self-determination that is the central theme of the published work.

Obviously, this shift in thematic focus reflects a major shift in perspective for McNickle, and it evolved from his recognition of the endurance of Native cultures and the inherent theme of self-determinism found in their verbal arts. This realization enlightened his revision of the manuscript. The changes he made brought him very close to the image of Native peoples he was to present in the remainder of his fiction, and also in the numerous anthropological works he produced. Far from romanticized and far from completely scientific, this image focuses on the lifeways, attitudes, and beliefs he found indelibly etched in their narratives.

There were other forces guiding him as well. A major breakthrough came for him when he began to understand the appeal and confusion his first drafts held for publishers. In October of 1934, he received the reports from the readers of yet another publishing house: Covici, Friede and Company. The reports suggest that, in this draft, McNickle makes too much of the missionary/Catholic conflict with the old Salish ways and too little of the conflict between "two civilizations." The publisher also calls for the softening of white characters who appear as "villains" and considers Archilde's final arrest too sudden: "The last two chapters need careful reworking to build consciously for the tragic implications of Archilde's failure which is, in a higher sense, at the same time his personal triumph over his own past."[4] By November, McNickle had a contract with this publisher, who agreed to produce 3,000 copies of the book—now entitled "Dead Grass"—in an initial printing.[5] By February of 1935, Covici and Friede retracted the contract. McNickle was not making significant progress in their direction. Why would a hungry, unpublished writer drag his feet?

The reports could not have been pleasing to McNickle for several reasons. First, as the allusion to Archilde's arrest attests, he had altered the earlier manuscript to satisfy the desire of his audience to read about the conflict between Anglo and Indian, but the publisher's readers did not recognize that the struggle between priest and Salish, between new and old, *was* indeed a conflict between "two civilizations." There is, of course, an added aspect to this response, as suggested by the readers' comments. The missionaries and "white characters" do not prevail; Western civilization does not win, although it does establish authority. Moreover, Archilde's sudden arrest has a very dramatic effect that emphasizes two conflicting perceptions of justice, an effect McNickle obviously desired but which the publisher did not find consistent with the development of the plot that culminates in it. But there are two plots leading to it, one Salish and one Anglo. The publishers saw only one. Finally, there is the confusion over Archilde's end, which the readers saw as "failure" but also a victory over "his own past." But which past, and in what way?

These questions may be impossible to answer because one cannot be certain that the manuscript read by Covici and Friede was identical to the published novel. But in light of the readers' comments, it appears to have been very similar. Their contract was withdrawn in February, and by November McNickle had a contract with Dodd and Mead, the book's publishers, so perhaps he did not alter it radically, given the lengthy process of manuscript reading and contract negotiations. Instead, he appears to have devoted his time to extensive reading at the Library of Congress, and most likely in tribal narratives, as his letter to Barbeau in July, asking for permission to use a story, substantiates. The revisions he made before November did not alter the plot of the book that Covici and Friede found interesting, but his changes certainly added to the substance of the novel.

In effect, *The Surrounded* is not a condemnation of white dominance as much as it is an affirmation of traditional Salish values, perceptions of order in the world, and ways to knowledge and power. This can be seen by looking past what would at first appear to be the central plot of the novel—the story of Warden Smith's death and the circumstances that lead directly to Archilde's dramatic arrest by Agent Parker. This plot remains from the original manuscripts, and it is used to address what became McNickle's ancillary purpose: to call attention to, and comment upon, the directions and circumstances of Indian/Euramerican relations, both past and present. But its characters are stereotypes similar to those found in popular fiction, and they need never be developed beyond their flat, self-involved natures to fulfill their political purpose. In this plot, borrowed from the written convention, Archilde plays an individual concerned with only one thing: his own, personal interests, at the expense of his relationship with his people. Sheriff Quigley is, simply stated, an old-West lawman; and Moser is a businessman. In short, each represents one of the compelling forces in the history of red/white relations—social, legal/political, economical—and their interaction does not contribute any fresh insights into the contemporary condition of Native cultures. Following the conventions of structure found in popular fiction about Indians, this plot is concerned more with the lack of justice in Archilde's arrest than with his development as a Salish tribal member.

Covici and Friede read the story of murder and arrest and took it to be the central plot. Despite their reservations about it, McNickle kept it in his final draft because it obviously appealed to his audience. It was something readers could recognize, something that fit their ideas about the current state of Indians and their cultures; but McNickle turned it to another purpose. He used the recognizable and acceptable to lead his reader away from a sympathetic reaction based upon a patronizing perception that Native cultures need help, and to an understanding that they need simply to be left alone to pursue their own futures, in ways they choose. In the novel there are also scenes and actions that tell of the relationship between Archilde and his people. These trace the steps in Archilde's education and intertwine his quest for the power of self-determination with the long history of a similar quest by the Salish, who also seek the knowledge of how to act in order to direct their future. The readers are witnesses to the crux: that moment in time when a transformation is about to occur, when well considered action must be taken. As McNickle demonstrates with the events of this Salish plot, Indians, including the Métis, have been in many such predicaments before, and yet have lived to create and tell stories about trying times and their resolutions.

Archilde's education is the central structuring device for the novel, as McNickle's letter to William Gates in 1934 attests. This is understandable, given the Salish respect for education shown in their stories, including the story of Amotken and the creation in which three races of people are destroyed because they refused to learn. Archilde is the pivotal point, the reader's point of view, between the two plots McNickle invents from two conflicting educations—one Anglo and one Salish—but it is the latter that ultimately concerns him. One way of presenting an accurate image of the Salish was to replicate the tenor of their oral literature. *The Surrounded* depicts traditional ways to knowledge; moreover, like similar characters in Native verbal arts, Archilde moves from a self-centered individual to one who has a very clear awareness of his relationship to his people and its attendant responsibilities.

Although Catharine played only a minor role in early drafts of the work, she figures prominently in the major plot of *The Surrounded*. As in the early, handwritten manuscript, the published work opens with Archilde's return to her, but it opens *in medias res*. McNickle chose to begin his final version of the narrative "in the middle," in motion, not with a lengthy expository passage. Also, the opening clearly emphasizes Archilde's relationship with his mother. When he comes home, he goes directly to her, rather than to his father who represents Euramerican attitudes. She and her cousin, Modeste, are Archilde's bridges to the past, and this initial loyalty reveals Archilde's dilemma; he has feelings for his mother and her people, but he is also strongly attracted to urban America and its easy life. The conflict between old and new ways is the thread that runs from the early draft, to the manuscript read by Covici and Friede, and finally to the published version itself, and it reflects the confusion of contemporary Salish and Native peoples in general. Significantly, in its final form, the tribal ties prevail.

In fact, Catharine's story has such a direct bearing upon Archilde's that the events of hers must be examined to understand the process of his education—its origins, directions, and implications.

Like Philomene, McNickle's mother, Catharine was born at a time of radical change. Philomene saw her people, the Métis, move from a powerful force on the northern plains to a race of homeless refugees, powerless and at the mercy of forces beyond their control. They had fought for their lands—and lost. McNickle recognized that the story of his family was similar to the story of the Salish and of Native peoples in general. The Salish, too, were at the mercy of powerful forces, and he explored the nature of these forces and the possible ways that they might be circumvented. His findings were quite radical, from the point of view of a Euramerican audience in 1936, yet conservative for a Native. To represent them in his novel he expanded the character of Catharine to present a focused, personal view of the history of Anglo/Salish relations. This purpose is similar to the one that gave birth to Max, Moser, and Quigley, only from the Salish perspective, and Catharine's character transcends this one simple role. She also demonstrates the ability of Native traditions to prevail over adversity, including the ill effects of European colonization. She is not a flat character.

The first event of Catharine's story is given quite early in *The Surrounded*, for it establishes her as the representation of the changes that have come about through the influence of the priests. McNickle provides this connection by making the arrival of the priests Catharine's earliest memory, the dawning of her awareness. Although he gives his reader three tellings of it, the first is by Catharine herself. Interestingly, her memory of it is sparked by a visit from Louis, her other son, who is a fugitive from white law. When she attempts to comprehend the reasons for his recent behavior, she is immediately transported to that point in her life—and the life of the Salish—that is associated with it:

> She rocked back and forth in the gloom, frightened and uncomfortable in the knowledge the priests had given her. She had been obedient to the fathers always. Her memory did not go beyond them, it began with them. It began that day at the end of summer when the missionaries came through the twisting defile which led from the Jocko River into the valley of Sniel-emen and planted their Cross. It went with her father to meet them and spread the blanket for

them. It heard her father speak. His words were unnamed birds to her; she heard them fly about but did not know them, yet this is what they said: "Now Kolinzuten has answered us, he has fulfilled us. We have long asked for black-robed teachers, they who have no wives, and who carry the cross. Thrice we have sent runners to St. Louis as all men know. Now, father, speak, and we will do as you tell us."[6]

As her body moves, going nowhere, her mind takes a journey into the past. She rocks between a way of life taught by the priests and one that marked her people as an active, powerful force in the world. And McNickle equates the difference in lifeways with a difference in knowledge: one distant and nostalgic, the other frightening, uncomfortable, immediate. Catharine gives the reader a picture of how it was before, as well as after, the priests emerged from "the twisting defile" of the Jocko River.

With this memory, Catharine pauses to question and to assess her situation, much as Sinchlep/Coyote does when he confronts evil in the story of "The Ram's Horn Tree." Like him, she wonders if she and her people have the power to survive the crisis, the dangers she sees around her. Like him, she will employ similar means to resolve this dilemma. She looks to the past. She asks which lifeway is preferable, which demonstrates the greater good and possibility for happiness, and McNickle clearly defines "good" in terms of Salish power, the potential for self-determination. Her journey into memory recounts, for nontribal readers, the act of a people consciously, deliberately, and communally attempting to determine their future by acquiring knowledge alien to their world.[7] We learn from Running Wolf, Catharine's father, that Kolinzuten—McNickle's name for Amotken, the creator in the Salish origin story—has sent the priests because the Salish have requested them and have taken an active part in their arrival by sending runners to St. Louis three times. The meeting Catharine remembers is the fourth attempt to bring them. One sees similar attempts to alter circumstances through trial-and-error methods in the oral stories. One also finds the four-step process, by which Amotken created the world and its beings and by which Sinchlep/Coyote taught the people the skills necessary to survive the archevil Amteep's attempts to destroy them. The duplication of motif and structure is hardly coincidental and implies a world view antithetical to the fatalistic notion of the Salish that McNickle exhibits in the earlier draft.

Interestingly, McNickle simultaneously emphasizes attitudes basic to Salish culture and remains objective and true to the "American" written historical record. The Salish actually sent three groups of runners to St. Louis, and one to the Green River rendezvous to collect Father De Smet on June 30, 1840.[8] McNickle sets the date at 1854, but the exact date is not as important as the actions he imagines taking place when they first met and the contradictory perceptions about power that those actions symbolize. Understandably, the two plots are born in the same point of time.

McNickle carefully underscores elements of Catharine's memory of the meeting that mark the significance of this event to the Salish. The gathering of the people, the spreading of the blanket, the soaring quality of Running Wolf's words, and the planting of the cross (implying an organic, growing event?) all build a sense of ceremonial importance. After all, community, ritual, and articulation are key aspects of ceremony and, therefore, enduring qualities of the cultures that McNickle saw persevering. In this instance—as in later instances—McNickle purposefully counterpoints the hope for renewal implicit in the ceremony with the imposition of a new order. The event is followed immediately by the Salish loss of identity; Catharine is baptized and renamed Catharine Le Loup and her father is renamed Gregoire. The world is being transformed but hardly along the lines expected by the Salish. A new way and a new language are supplanting the old, and the priests' words of promised happiness for those who accept them carry back into Catharine's present where she looks "upon a chaotic world—so many things dead, so many words for which she knew no meaning; her sons developing into creatures such as had never lived in her childhood . . ." (22).

The priests' arrival is the initial event in her story, and her memory of it initiates her attempt to reconcile what she has been taught by the priests with what she sees and feels and fears. The memory also provides the basis for the interpretation of subsequent events—a new way of reading the plot, and perhaps history, for those who believe that Native cultures' fates were sealed from the first moment of contact with the European.

McNickle uses the coincidence between Salish tradition and Euramerican historical record to evolve two opposing perceptions of events. The Jesuit fathers are teachers, and, given the Salish respect for teachers and the emphasis placed on learning throughout their oral literature, this title ensures the priests' acceptance and undisputed power. In fact, the term "father" is often synonymous with leader or "chief" in the Salish language.[9] McNickle's irony hinges, of course, on his readers' awareness of the results the Salish hope to achieve with the meeting. The priests' instruction is meant to give the people new actions, new movements, or new ceremonies to counter the ill effects of the European incursion. The people go to their antagonists for the knowledge of how to react to them, just as did Sinchlep/Coyote in verbal arts and just as did Philomene when she adopted the patterns of Euramerican written rhetoric for her letter to the Bureau of Indian Affairs. As Running Wolf says, "Father, speak, and we will do. . . ." However, the new teachings the Salish seek are meant to work within a traditional Salish framework; Catharine accepts the priests' teachings and ceremonies, but with them, over time, come radical changes in her way of life. The coincidences between what the people hope for (the arrival of the priests and their agreement to teach the people) and what they see happen seem to indicate, initially, that their actions have been successful. Of course, readers with even a rudimentary knowledge of American history realize that the priests try to destroy Salish culture and create a new one in their own image.

McNickle uses three tellings of their arrival to repeat simple, crucial questions. For many, the old Salish cultural framework seems to be a thing of the past, but is it? Do the old powers and values survive, despite the new, the modern? To limit the possibility that readers might answer inappropriately, McNickle provides, quite early, a brief comparison of and judgment upon the two cultural perceptions. It comes after the reader has shared Catharine's memory of the priests' arrival but before the second telling of the same event by Father Grepilloux. First, McNickle gives the Salish point of view, then the comparison of two ways of perceiving the altered world—clearly and unequivocally stated in the narrator's description of the town of St. Xavier—then the Euramerican perspective of the initial meeting of priest and Salish. By the time of the second telling, McNickle wants his readers to have developed a heightened critical sense about history—events and their meanings—and thereby to question their own beliefs about the endurance and integrity of Native cultures. There can be no doubt about the author's idea of the priests' influence once he has described St. Xavier, for the town epitomizes the nature of the change that took place in the valley of Sniel-emen with the planting of the cross.

St. Xavier belongs to two eras: modern commercial America and the "primitive past" (narrator's words) of the Salish. For his modern readers, McNickle first describes the Anglo side of town with its recognizable order of sidewalks and flower beds and its hidden outhouses; the description of the "hovels" of Indiantown stands in sharp contrast. It is a scene an Anglo reader of early writings about Indians would probably expect. In fact, it resembles the descriptions Thoreau gives of Indian communities in *The Maine Woods*, but McNickle infuses the image with new meaning (and with irony) by demonstrating the unwillingness of the Euramerican mind to perceive an order behind the squalor:

> The newcomers [the European immigrants] thought Indiantown had been built without a plan, but they were wrong. There had been a plan, even if it didn't lend itself to street construction and regularity. Each cabin faced the church. Each door—there were no windows—gave a full view of God's tall house and the cropped poplar trees around it. The newcomers saw only the confusion. (35)

The plan follows no rigid design imposed from without, no European "construction and regularity." Instead, it demonstrates the Salish awareness that the world has its own, mutable order and that human designs must continuously conform to it. The Salish understand that their survival depends upon their ability to recognize the shifting powers that move in the world and to align themselves appropriately. Their doors face the church because the priests have been given the power to direct the future of the Salish; the sole entrance to their dwellings faces, and therefore acknowledges by opening to, this new source of power in their world.

The Europeans' idea of order, as McNickle demonstrates it, is restrictive and ethnocentric. It separates the world into two realms—the material and the spiritual—insisting that the two are distinct yet inseparable. When they find another cultural sense of order at work, they see only "squalor," a term denoting a material state that, for them, is synonymous with internal character (i.e., spiritual) deficiencies. Their vision is blind to any other perception of the world, and their place in it, for its scientific, geometrical sense of regularity is arrogantly myopic and, therefore, inflexible. McNickle sees that inflexibility as a weakness. Like the mountain sheep who saw only what he wanted to see and was therefore destroyed by Sinchlep, or the Foolish Folk the Salish found in the valley when they arrived who acted out of their own selfish interests and became extinct, the newcomers may ultimately find themselves at the mercy of forces that can move the world through sweeping transformations, forces that are beyond their comprehension and, therefore, their control. The Salish, however, have survived radical changes before, and they may even endure the incursion of the European. As McNickle says of Indiantown, it "was left to itself, but not out of mercy. Its lack of plan and of sanitation saved it" (35). All the Salish in the novel—and perhaps all Native peoples—desire one thing: to be left alone to see to their own lives and futures. Although surrounded, they still live, and with life comes the possibility of working another change.

After the two world views are established by their perceptions of St. Xavier, McNickle gives the second telling of the meeting between the Salish and the priests: two perceptions of place, two of event. The diary of Father Grepilloux, who was one of the first priests to arrive in the valley, adds further detail to Catharine's brief account of that day, and the detail is revealing. The fact that McNickle chose to present one "telling" from memory and one from a written record is also important. His own quest for understanding took him into two traditions—into the oral as well as the written—and his conclusions about their relative strengths can be found here. Catharine's sense of history is a living, dynamic process that ultimately will allow her to understand the correct relationship between the event and her life—and the life of her people. She will learn how to act in light of that knowledge. Father Grepilloux, on the other hand, resigns his attempts to understand the meaning of the event to the recording of his memories in a static artifact. Actually, he reads it to Max, Catharine's Euramerican husband, because he can no longer be sure of his memory of the event; he wants Max to add his impressions of the early years—the Indians then as opposed to now. Interestingly, he asks the same question Catharine asks: what good has come from the priests' teachings? As he looks around him, he sees the dissolution and corruption that she has already noted. (Ironically, such memoirs reinforce, rather than alter, social attitudes; Catharine's, however, is revolutionary.)

The irony of this sad figure trying to justify a life of work and dedication lies in the fact that Grepilloux has acted out of the best intentions. He has literally given his life, in true Christian fashion, to improving the lives of his "less fortunate brothers." The bias of his perception is implicit in his early belief that the Salish were less fortunate because they did not possess what he considered to be of value; they lacked material ease and they were not Christian. Despite his kind and sensitive ministrations, his actions doom the people he has hoped to "save" from the evil of their misguided ways. In this way he is like those Anglo authors McNickle mentions in his letter to Gates who want to help "save" the cultures of Indian peoples by writing down their stories, just as Grepilloux records the story of "Big Paul." They both succeed "only in making the uplifters ridiculous and sinking the victim into deeper obscurity."[10] There is only one thing that Grepilloux hopes might balance the evil effects on the Salish: "Of course . . . they have God" (59). His Christian beliefs were born of another place, and they have remained unchanged—albeit weakened by doubt—after nearly sixty years of life in a new landscape. Inflexibly, unwaveringly, they have dictated his actions and the way he saw this new world. Like the mountain sheep in the story of the Ram's Horn tree, he follows this limited perception to his own loss. Grepilloux has unquestioningly followed the commands to do battle with all pagan influences; now his Christian sense of order blinds his attempts to address the damage his battles have wrought.

And the same blindness is recorded in his diary. Father Grepilloux's telling of the meeting focuses on those elements important
to him because of their novelty or their Christian implications. In
style, McNickle pays close heed to the early writings that record
Father De Smet's first encounter with the Salish, and the flowery
prose is purposefully similar to other accounts of "explorers" that
McNickle came across in his research. To the young Grepilloux,
Running Wolf is a "Great Chief, a Patriarchal man," and his eagle
wing the "Symbol of his Office." Likewise, the people gathered are a
"large Company" (46). The style emphasizes specific aspects of the
event but also the gravity of occurrences that day. In fact, the
publisher, E. H. Dodd Jr., removed the "archaic capitalization," and
McNickle wrote a letter demanding that it be replaced.[11] The style
certainly brings Grepilloux's perception of the event into clear contrast with Catharine's, which is understated by comparison. In her
story, her father is the "chief of his branch of the Salish people" (21).
She does not mention an eagle wing; its presence would be taken
for granted. Through such discrepancies, the reader begins to realize
that each character comes to the meeting with his or her own set of
cultural imperatives. Each has a clear idea of what is taking place,
but the ideas are obviously antithetical.

Which does McNickle want us to believe to be "factual," or more
closely adhering to what actually transpired that day? Memory or
diary, imagination or history? Which do we accept as an accurate
record of the forces that were at work in this event? Although
Grepilloux recognizes the solemnity of the occasion, he perceives in
it the hand of his god: "I thought they understood perfectly what
this moment meant to them, and that in their hearts, they were
praising the Author of their Beings" (47). As McNickle has already
shown, the Salish *are* praising the author of their being, and his
name is Kolinzuten. They praise him because their efforts have
resulted in what appears to be success; the priests have come.
Grepilloux also sees the workings of his god in the Salish willingness
to accept his teachings. He cannot conceive of another force—their
own traditions—at work. The two contradictory perceptions of
what is taking place are further emphasized by the priest's record of
Running Wolf's words, as translated by a man named Ignace. "We
[the Salish] have been worshipping False Gods, and we want you to

teach us the True God" (47). The style and tone conform to the rest of Grepilloux's memoir, but how does one account for the discrepancy between this rendition of what was said and Catharine's? In hers, Running Wolf says that the priests' coming is the direct result of Kolinzuten's influence; he has answered their prayers. The implications of the two accounts are, literally, worlds apart. Catharine's reflects Salish tradition; Grepilloux's condemns that tradition and proffers another. Has the priest altered the meaning, or did Ignace translate incorrectly?

Either way, Grepilloux's account of the meeting has become suspect, and we begin to doubt written history and to accept oral. His misinterpretation of the Salish eagerness and the biased slant given to Running Wolf's words are echoed at his memoir's end where he reports the chief's attempt to present his eagle wing to Father Lamberti—the fictional equivalent of Father De Smet—who heads the expedition. The act is symbolic, one recognizes, of the Salish transference of leadership (teachership), but Lamberti refuses and the Salish are disappointed. What one infers, and what the priests miss, is that the ceremony begun with the gathering of the people and the spreading of the blanket has not been completed. One senses the dissatisfaction, and this sense is heightened by Lamberti's explanation that the priests "would not interfere in temporal matters, and wished nothing of them but to be allowed to minister to their Spiritual Health" (47). Readers versed in Christian tradition might easily accept the priest's separation between body and spirit, the physical and spiritual realms, but, if they have been attentive and sensitive to the Salish attitudes presented thus far in the novel, they must recognize the cultural basis for the distinction between two domains. For the Salish in *The Surrounded*, "physical" ill health is "spiritual" in nature, and so is its cure.

The final telling of the priests' arrival furnishes the relationships needed to resolve the ambiguities in the two previous renditions and the perceptions they display. The power of Modeste's version lies in his ability to develop the significance of the priests beyond the personal exploration of Catharine and to place it in a historical context inaccessible to Father Grepilloux. His account of the episode is very brief, because it is only one event in a larger narrative: the life journey of the Salish people. Modeste places the priests against the background of Salish verbal history, thus providing the communal view, his cultural perspective. First came the flint arrowhead, then the iron ax, and then the white man's gun. There have been many steps, and many individual stories, in the process that leads to the meeting. However, the last implement, the gun, altered the very nature of the world. Death, fear, and mistrust—all the things Catharine sees in her world after sixty years of Christianity—garnered greater shares of Salish attention, and thus directed their thoughts and actions. It is this state of affairs that leads the Salish on a search for "the new thing," the teachings of the priests that will counter this evil influence.

Modeste's telling also notes that the Salish heard of the priests from some Iroquois refugees who had been adopted by the tribe. This is historically accurate, and it is interesting to note that one of these men—Old Ignace, as he was called—had already converted to Catholicism. One account places his son, Baptiste, in a Catholic seminary.[12] A further irony emerges, once again, from the juxtaposition of historical fact with Salish tradition. The eagerness of the Salish to learn has led them to two traditional ways to knowledge, learning from a trusted individual and communal reason and discussion, but these have been subverted, a trust has been broken. Ignace mediates for the two parties and, as his translation of Running Wolf's words indicates, he is fully aware of what the priests want to hear. Historically, he took an active role in persuading the Salish to summon the priests, no doubt because he was Catholic himself and wanted his new religion to spread among his adopted tribe. Once again, noble sentiments result in misguided actions and disastrous effects.

With Modeste's story, one begins to see a pattern taking form, but, once the old man takes his audience to the meeting, he pauses, leaving his listeners at that distant point in the past, wrapped in their attempts to understand its significance. The old man is a good storyteller. He mumbles "Ies choopminzin," which McNickle translates as the traditional Salish cap to a story: "I stop talking to you" (74). It is important that McNickle does not have Modeste end the story but merely stop talking to allow thoughtful reflection, by characters and readers alike. This way the story lives on in contemporary life; the device highlights the fact that its end has yet to be determined. McNickle's "telling" follows verbal convention, tying the story of the priests to the Salish canon. Like older stories, this one relates an error in judgment and the need to correct it, and the stories of Catharine and Archilde provide the means.

The Surrounded focuses on one crucial segment of recent Salish history: the time since the advent of the European. McNickle's major concern is, after all, the survival of tribal cultures, using his own family history (the Métis diaspora) and his experience with the Salish as representative of the continuation and articulation of tribal identity despite trying times. The priests' arrival is, in his estimation, inextricably tied to the diminished power of the Salish, and, although it supposedly took place sixty years prior, it is the first event in the novel, the one that leads to events particular to the life stories of the other characters. Moreover, like the Salish, McNickle's narrative draws no distinctions between the material and spiritual realms of experience; when he explains their loss, he presents the various agents who worked to bring it about—priest and settler, lawman and businessman—as manifestations of one force. Guided by greed, Moser and his kind bring changes to the valley that compound those brought about by Grepilloux or Max, whose motives are supposedly less mercenary. Like the opening of Pandora's box, one event gives birth to many related and detrimental occurrences.

Catharine's feast is the second major event in the novel, and it is interesting that McNickle does not allow direct, "outside" interference during this Salish custom. Although they are not forgotten, Max and the Euramerican world he represents are not invited. Instead, McNickle constructs a scene and mood that are purposefully suggestive of precolonial times. Here one finds the comfort and warmth of close family ties; meat cooks on open fires; women provide a communal center, with gossip and jokes. The Salish language a murmur in the background, the venerable Modeste sits "smoking and waiting for the women to serve the meat, his sightless eyes blinking to his thoughts" (61). But this is not some ancient camp. It is set in modern America, circa 1914, the years when the young McNickle heard the stories and songs he would remember later as he created this fictional event. And these were the years when the Salish realized the extent to which they were surrounded, and the old ways endangered. In fact, Archilde insists that the old way of life is dead. For the young man, and perhaps the readers, the feast seems nothing more than a relic from the past. But it is a crucial relic.

Archilde is initially resentful about having to attend the feast because it thrusts him directly into the center of a way of life he had turned his back on the year before by retreating into the white world that surrounds the reservation. As he notes, nothing has changed in that year, and so his resolution to make this his last visit home stiffens. However, his trip home is more than a simple leave-taking. He has come to absorb some last impressions of people and place, memories to accompany him when he leaves, for good, to be assimilated into the mainstream of American society. Such is his dream. However, this need for one last contact betrays an affinity for his people and home that he has been taught to deny by the priests in the mission school and the teachers at Chemawa. Perhaps like McNickle himself, Archilde must force his attachments "underground" and align his attitudes and actions with those acceptable to the society in which he has chosen to live. Paradoxically, his resignation to leave the seemingly changeless, hence (in his belief) pointless, reservation life provides the emotional state of mind necessary for his reinitiation into Salish ways. His journey does not end; it begins with his homecoming. Like a man on a traditional quest for a vision, his isolation and detachment bring him closer to his people.

By the time of the final draft, McNickle recognized how Native cultures survive, despite the odds against them. His description of the feast, and the ways that he presents the stories that are told at it, depict the dynamics of Salish culture and experience at work. Slowly, Archilde becomes enmeshed in the process of the evening, for it has a power that draws him along. The people eat and then relax. The stories begin, and, in the telling, one finds how fully McNickle understood the cultures of his youth.

The first story is told by an old woman who has lost most of her teeth. The loss, a physical restriction, leads to the distortion of some sounds, "but the story was an old one and nothing was lost" (64). McNickle states quite clearly that the oral process survives, despite restrictions, impediments, and loss. The people are still able to share, communally, in stories that define ways to knowledge, to self-determination, and to survival.

The woman tells the story of Coyote and Flint, and McNickle's rendition of the tale says a great deal about his idea of the power of spoken stories and the problems with written ethnographies. In fact, in one letter to William Gates, he says he was trying to write some Mayan verse after reading a few in a journal. However, he stopped because of a sudden realization:

> I was perhaps contemplating doing the very thing which, in reading, I have distrusted and felt antagonized by: I mean those "translations" one finds of Indian poetry in which the "translator" has made the Indian singer over into a kind of sonneteer or at worst a *vers lyricist* [last word smudged], and on top of that has asked us to admire the individuality of Indian poetry.[13]

This sentiment was to be echoed again and again by tribal writers over the ensuing decades, but his words also include an insight about the problems of rendering verbal texts to the written word and of alien literary traditions. He had to solve these problems, and to do so he drew upon his own experiences with verbal arts to reverse the effects of collection and translation.

McNickle found the story of Flint, as he acknowledges in a prefatory note to the novel, in Helen Fitzgerald Sanders' *Trails Through Western Woods*, but his "telling" of it is quite different.[14] Why did he alter the way it was produced in his source? In a letter to his agent, Ruth Rae, written only a few months before publication, McNickle discusses the need to get permission from Sanders, and from Barbeau, for the stories he intends to use. Of the story of Flint he says: "The tale is authentic, hence my interest in using it. . . . It is difficult to see how a myth or folktale can be copyrighted, especially when it comes so close to yourself as this does to me."[15] He obviously had a first-hand acquaintance with this story, one that enlightened the changes he made in it when he incorporated it into his novel. The sense that guided him becomes clear when the two versions are compared.

One obvious difference between the two lies in voice, as created by sentence complexity. Sanders repeatedly uses long, compound sentences: strings of brief clauses joined by "and." The result is a quality suggestive of a hasty, childlike narrative against which her own formal, flowery prose stands in clear relief. Whether or not she purposely manipulated the material is unimportant here. What is significant is McNickle's refusal to reproduce it exactly as she presented it. Instead, he opts for short, simple sentences that give his narrative a dramatic, vocal quality by alternating verbalization with moments of silence that isolate and thereby clarify actions by allowing time for reflection and visualization: "It was like this. He [Coyote] had nothing to put on his arrow. He had just bark and you can see that would not go through a buffalo" (64). Actions are also differentiated into paragraphs for a similar purpose.

The use of the second person is also McNickle's choice, and it evokes a direct relationship between teller and listener, or reader. He adds humor, a quality often ignored in early ethnographies concerned with recording the last, therefore grave, gasps of dying cultures. When the old woman in the novel describes Coyote's pointless arrow, McNickle has her exhibit traditional narrative license, for teller and novelist alike. She moves from the perspective of a narrator telling a story into that of a buffalo being shot with an ineffectual arrow, thus illustrating while adding her own personal touch: "Now I will eat that fly if he doesn't go away" (64). Finally, McNickle even gives the feeling of the old woman's animation as she tells of the fight between Coyote and Flint. "Then they were fighting and going this way and that way . . ." (64). One can imagine her rocking movement as her chin points out the directions in which their fight takes them. These alterations and additions give the telling a vigor, a life, not present in Sanders's work, and a power more closely representative of an actual storytelling event. It becomes less an artifact and more a living thing.

Like a traditional storyteller, McNickle draws his readers into an active participation in events by engaging their imaginations on several levels at once. First, he asks his readers to visualize, perhaps even sensualize, an evening's setting: the sounds and smells and tastes. Then, he challenges them to interpret stories that seem, at least initially, to derive from times long past but, it is implied, are relevant to today and to Archilde. This demonstrates McNickle's awareness of what more recent scholars have only begun to explore in the last twenty years: that Native verbal arts are more than mere statements of information. They represent a dynamic, complex process that works simultaneously on many planes of experience.[16] By combining his own understanding of verbal traditions with the written records of oral stories, McNickle was able to instill his narrative with the strengths of each. His novel is a written record, of sorts, that retells Sanders's story but also creates a Native voice to tell it. He performed the story but also gave it a context. He knew what had to remain, if the story was to be "authentic" and its original purpose perpetuated.

In the story, the specifics of Coyote's journey after Flint are described elaborately. McNickle could easily have excised such repetitive detail, but not without altering the story's effect. When the repetition is closely considered, readers come upon what appears to be a discrepancy. Fox tells Coyote that Flint passed by three days prior to Coyote's own arrival. How does one account for the fact that Coyote camps in the same places Flint camped yet is still able to overtake him? If we attempt to answer this riddle, we reach the unsatisfying, illogical conclusion that either Coyote passed other camps or that Flint spent more than one day at a camp. The storyteller does not note either detail. If readers recognize, however, that Coyote follows his prey's movements exactly, that he overtakes him on the fourth day, and that he chooses to wait patiently for Flint to come to him rather than attack him immediately from behind, they find another logic at work: the logic of appropriate movement. Coyote moves beyond the strictures of time and space that limit characters in many narrative canons, and his concern for correct form gives him a power by which distance traveled and time expended become fluid to his purpose. The ambiguities between the actions of Flint and Coyote call attention to the process followed by Coyote, and the listeners/readers learn, through their conscious effort to retrace the journey and to resolve the discrepancies, that deliberate and well considered actions are more important and more powerful than physical barriers. In short, the actions of the storyteller and the character of Coyote provide the story's message. Its end result, the advent of the arrowhead, is simply the humorous medium.

All the people benefit from the efforts of the storyteller to relate literature to the present. As McNickle carefully depicts, the telling draws Modeste's people closer together as they share a moment of similar response:

> When the story was told everybody laughed. It was a very old
> story, the kind grandmothers told to grandchildren, and it always
> made people laugh. Archilde had not intended to listen, yet he had
> heard every word. The story had amused him in spite of himself. It
> left a spark of gay remembrance in his mind. (66)

Obviously, he responds despite his pessimism and reluctance to become a part of his family's life. He cannot resist the attraction inherent in the stories and the process of their telling. As with Catharine's record of the priests' arrival, memory provides the central, powerful force in bridging the gulf between an individual and a people, a past and a present. At the feast, it is the focal point between the gathered individuals. Even Archilde remembers fondly the telling of such stories in his own past, and the amusement felt by the people evolves from more than the humor inherent in the story. They laugh because each shares with those near the old lessons learned from such stories in the past. As children, they learned from the oral process of verbal arts, and it is implied—through the effects of the evening on those gathered—that the process may still teach them.

Moreover, McNickle describes Archilde's reaction to the story as a spark; of course, fires emerge from sparks, and fires illuminate. It is also interesting to note this use of light in the original manuscript. The change in McNickle's attitude between the two drafts is apparent. In the first, the spark of dawning awareness comes at book's end, and it is incomplete and undeveloped. Here it comes very early to mark the initiation of the process that will result in Archilde's integration into his tribe. An afterthought has become a central thread of the book.

The second story is told by an old man named Whitey. One of McNickle's sources for the story is *Indian Days in the Canadian Rockies* by Marius Barbeau, but personal experience is another. He notes in a letter to Barbeau that this story is found with the Kutenai also.[17] As with the earlier story, there are a number of changes that McNickle makes that tell a great deal about his understanding of Native texts and their performance. The most obvious and significant of these is the addition of the dream. In Barbeau's account, the protagonist of the story, Maloolek, hears of the iron ax by rumor.[18] The inclusion of a dream changes the whole complexion of the story, for it gives the old man's actions (or inaction in this case) a devout patience that echoes Coyote's in the earlier story of Flint (and patience is a quality sorely lacking in Archilde). In his dream the old man has been told that his people must "watch out and not let this thing that was to make life easy escape their notice" (66). Only the old man remains attentive, despite the time involved and the derision of his people. He trusts in the power of personal vision, and it is by his perseverance that his people gain this new tool. In this sense, McNickle's change in the protagonist's name becomes important as well. At first, he is referred to simply as an old man, but as the story evolves, he becomes Old Man. He shares the name of Old Man of the Sky from the story of the creation of the red and white races, and he is a benefactor also. The story of a "realistic" or historical character evolves into one of mythical proportions. For a time the old man adopts, through his carefully considered actions, the character of a supranatural being who can alter the shape of his world.

Again, Archilde's reactions to the story are carefully noted: "He wondered at it. And the more he reflected on it the more wonderful it grew. A story like that, he realized, was full of meaning" (69). Archilde's reactions challenge readers to look for the story's meaning—beyond the simple recounting of a piece of historical information. The Salish in the story benefit only through the faith and dedication the old man shows for one of the traditional ways to knowledge: through dream/vision. They have the ax but, more importantly, a valuable lesson. The story tells Archilde and his people to pay attention to the old ways, for through them power may be maintained. The world changes, so they must always be ready to act. By understanding the ways that people in the past found the knowledge necessary to respond to change, they can find resolutions to their own present quandaries.

Other stories are told in the night, but it is Modeste—the respected old man and heir to Running Wolf's chieftainship—who tells the final one. Although his story fits into the natural, chronological, and thematic progression in the stories of the evening, it at first seems very different. It seems "historical" rather than "mythical." It does not seem a folktale or legend or myth. In Modeste's words:

"These stories make the heart light. . . . My story will have to be a different one. I will tell it for this boy [Archilde] who has just come home after traveling out to the world. You have just heard him say that those old days are dead and won't come again. And it's true. But let me tell this story so he will see better just what it was like back in those times." (69)

The old man's words anticipate, exactly, the effect the story will have on his nephew. Modeste is reinitiating Archilde's education, as is the duty of an uncle in Salish tradition. Through Modeste's telling of the coming of the gun and then the cross, the young man "sees" for the first time the changes that came about in the world with the arrival of the European. These are changes that have had a direct bearing upon who he is and how he acts, even though the events that brought them about took place a long time before he was born.

First came the gun. "It was a different world from that time," as Modeste tells us (71). Clashes with old enemies like the Blackfeet and Crow became even more bitter as the number of men killed increased with the new, efficient weapon. The traditional means of affirming family and community ties and venting anger became too costly; the old balances like revenge gave way to new feelings of ineffectualness and, more importantly, fear. It was more than the fear of death, Modeste tells him; it was the fear of genocide. To counter these changes in the world, the Salish moved to find a new *somesh*, a new power. Ironically, they found the priests and their cross, and, rather than dispelling the fear, the new teachers used it to force their beliefs on the Salish. The decline of traditional ways and values came even more rapidly under the direction of the Jesuits.

One is given a bleak account with Modeste's history lesson, but it is not unqualified, just as the bleak statement some people see in *The Surrounded* is not unqualified. The feast has its positive aspects. The verbal arts, as McNickle shows us, are not dead. They have been a significant, compelling force throughout the evening. Through their power, Archilde has moved from a detached, belligerent observer to an active, involved participant. His arrogance and aloofness—the result of trying to align himself with the world "outside," with the world of the priests—dissolve because of the event, the process that brings Archilde back to an awareness of his people. They become "real" to him, and his "stiffness" against them dies. The last image of him in the night is telling: "He sat and thought about it [Modeste's story] and the flames shot upward and made light on the circle of black pines" (74). Once again, the image of illumination suggests Archilde's state.

This picture echoes that of Modeste at the beginning of the evening when the old man sat waiting for the meat to cook and considered, it is implied, what he was going to contribute to the evening. It also marks the end result of the storytelling that began with the first story's effect on Archilde, the "gay remembrance" that united him with his family. Modeste's thoughts and perceptions have become his nephew's. The Salish see with more than eyes as they consider the stories; imagination and memory are equally visionary, and McNickle repeatedly uses fire to describe the flash of insights that emerge from the meeting of the two ways of seeing. This intuitive spark shared by Archilde, Modeste, and the others at the feast becomes a full flame, shedding light on the surrounding darkness.

The evening has been a communal exploration and rediscovery of what was and what can be, through a shared oral literature and its tools—memory and imagination. All the stories are related to, and provide the continuity for, Salish experience, and Modeste's story is not, after all, so different from the others. It shares a similarity of purpose and effect. The "mythical" and "historical" realities of the Salish are not distinct, different. Both direct the thoughts and actions of Archilde and his people; both provide necessary information to help Archilde make crucial decisions. This melding of a literary canon with the stories of individuals allows the continuation of culture, and this blending of old and "new" is a characteristic of storytelling events, but also of McNickle's narratives. It is also found in the works of several recent Native American novelists and is therefore another mark of McNickle's innovative style.[19]

The first event in the novel is defined by the actions of the people: the merging of individuals into a community through a shared purpose and process during the ceremonial gathering to welcome the priests. McNickle gives the event a physical, temporal form in the character of Catharine; the event lives in, and through, her. She does not *symbolize* it, as one would expect in the context of other novels from the Euramerican traditions. She *is* the event, literally living the new knowledge achieved through the gathering; her story is the story of the alterations brought by the priests. She becomes the singular, focal point of power, the embodiment of the actions that are supposed to rebalance the forces of the world, just as individual characters in the old stories embody new *somesh*, new ceremonies for their people. Coyote and the old man in the story of the ax take active, beneficial roles in shaping the future of the people, and they transform the world through a close adherence to, and patient regard for, correct form and movement. Catharine is a similar force in this recent transformation with its new forms and movements: the rituals of the church and its dictates concerning behavior. The benefits, however, are open to debate.

Catharine's patience is worn thin by the lack of good her actions bring. Instead of happiness and ease and endurance—the results of Coyote's and Old Man's stories—she finds sadness and chaos and threats to survival. As Modeste admits, the old days are dead, but that is in the nature of things. Days come and go and things change. The world is dynamic, mutable and, although time may pass, the ways through which the Salish of the past dealt with continual change still exist. Perhaps another deliberate transformation is warranted. McNickle pits the effectiveness of the old ways—the endurance of ten thousand years—against the forces of the modern world. It is small wonder that Covici and Friede objected to his portrayal of that conflict—and that he refused to deemphasize it. Instead, he uses Catharine's story and Archilde's reinitiation into Salish lifeways to depict the durabiltiy of Salish culture. He begins the process at Catharine's feast, and it reaches its peak in the Dance, the central event for all the Salish of the novel.

The Dance takes place approximately one year after Archilde's homecoming, ironically on July Fourth, Independence Day. The world of the main characters has changed drastically in that year. Father Grepilloux and Max are dead, and Archilde has inherited his father's fortune. Also, Louis and Warden Smith are dead as a result of their meeting in the mountains on the deer-hunting trip, and they certainly are not forgotten by Sheriff Quigley who single-mindedly searches for Smith's grave, or by Catharine who has spent the winter trying to understand the meaning of what has happened. Moreover, Narcisse and Mike, Archilde's nephews, have returned from mission school and Mike is plagued by the fear the priests instill in their students. The world and the narrative have reached an important juncture for many individuals, as well as for a people. The old generation is dying; what will come with the new? McNickle has carefully prepared the ground for the Dance—and for attempts to answer that question.

Although Archilde recognizes the basis of Mike's illness, he cannot cure it. He tries the only way he knows, by attempting to rationalize away the boy's fear. But Mike's nightmares continue, frightening everyone in the house. Reasoning will not work because it is the product of the priests' logic: their world of regularity and their perception of order. Mike's is not a rational disease, as Archilde well knows. He, too, has been ill with it as a child in the mission school, and it still haunts him although he thinks he understands and controls it.

Early in the novel, he finds himself alone in the mission church. Curious, he steps behind the altar on the pretext of examining a painting and, despite his skill at intellectually dismissing the heaven and hell, the God and devil, used by the priests to ensure compliance in their congregation, he is overpowered by fear when a bat drops from behind the picture as he reaches to touch it. It is revealing to note here an earlier passage in which the bats flying through a beautiful, serene evening have the opposite effect (16). Place and its associations power Archilde's reactions, and in the realm of the priests, in their place, he is at their mercy. He needs to have faith in a rationale, an idea of order and power vastly different from theirs. If he hopes to be rid of their influence forever, he must become responsive to another set of associations and relationships that will help him interpret events in his life. In a word, he needs his own *somesh*. Indeed, Archilde, Mike, Catharine, and all the Salish need the same thing, and, when Archilde travels to visit Modeste, a recognizable pattern begins to take shape. By remembering Catharine's tale of the priests and the narrator's description of St. Xavier, readers can begin to employ a logical system based upon Salish imperatives in their interpretation of scenes.

McNickle uses Archilde's ride to reiterate:

> Since that evening of feasting almost a year ago, Archilde had not
> seen the old man, but he was frequently thinking of him and of the
> story he had told that night. Modeste's story about the old days was
> the first one, and he had heard many, that Archilde had listened to
> with his mind. It was the first story about his people that he under-
> stood. He could not explain why he had listened and understood,
> but since it had happened he was continually thinking about this
> old chief. (194)

The man who had, a year before, returned for a brief visit before
leaving his land for good has become engaged in his people's life. A
story has been working on him for a year, and his attitudes about his
kin have changed. They—people and story—now enter his
thoughts, demanding attention in positive ways he has never experienced. And, although McNickle is describing the reactions of a
fictional character, the changes he crafts and the bases for them
could apply equally to himself. No longer does his desire to portray
his people objectively lead to his misinterpretation of their physical/
spiritual condition. Instead, he sees beyond their lack of material
wealth and ease and turns this lack to a new purpose: to affirm
rather than condemn.

Modeste's camp is an odd blend of past and present. A new, frame
house stands near a log cabin and a tepee. McNickle's statement is
clear. The old structures have not been abandoned for the comforts
of the new. Instead, the new have been used selectively; the house is
used for sleeping quarters, but without modern beds, while the
others are used as kitchen, storage, and so on. As with his description of St. Xavier, McNickle uses the old man's camp to illustrate two
perceptions of reservation material life:

> There is a kind of chaos about an Indian's homestead that, however
> complete and hopeless, is nevertheless not inherent; it does not be-
> long to the man. In the tepee, everything is in place; but when
> houses are built and farming implements acquired, then nothing is
> surprising. . . . (195)

In the camp an order and logic are at work that are predicated upon
traditional use patterns. The seeming squalor has come with the

intrusion of foreign ways of responding to the land and from the limitations placed upon a once free people. Chaos is in the eyes of the outsider. McNickle's goal is to take his readers on the inside to show the inherent qualities of Native Americans through the perception of Archilde, the young man who is receiving an education and reinitiation into his people's lifeways.

Throughout the interview, Archilde—originally the epitome of the modern, assimilated Indian—closely and respectfully follows age-old social customs, and old Modeste is pleased with the change he sees in his nephew: "His [Archilde's] greeting, spoken with reserve, raised a quick smile and a soft word from the old chief" (197). In Salish tradition, uncles are responsible for their nephews' guidance, and from an early age Archilde has received important gifts, including a "safe-keeper," from his. They share an important bond. After smoking, Archilde patiently waits for the old man to begin. When he speaks, Modeste simultaneously proposes a solution to Mike's problem and directs Archilde in his responsibilites to his own nephew. The tradition continues, despite Archilde's ignorance of or inability to perform his obligations.

At the feast the summer before, Modeste's words took us beyond the confusing realities of the present and the individual, to the clarity of the past and the communal. Here his words do the same. He tells Archilde, before the young man has a chance to broach the subject, that he has considered Mike's illness and it worries him a great deal because "if the children have this sickness, what will the old people be like in times to come? That is what I think about" (198). As the narrator carefully points out, Modeste sees fear as an illness, a disease threatening to his people's future. His interpretation of the young boy's behavior is hardly logical, from a Western medical point of view, but, for a man who makes no distinction between physical behavior and spiritual causes, the diagnosis makes sense. Moreover, its accuracy is underscored by his proposed cure, a cure from past traditions:

> "As you know, I have been without eyes for a long time and you know how I go about. My grandchild walks in front, holding a thong, and I follow. Now, it will be a good thing if Mike comes to this dance, to hear of the old times and dance with us who lived in

those days. If he wishes, and you let him, he shall take the place of
my grandson and lead me by the string." (199)

The ceremony will bind the generations, and this bonding will
provide the antibody to the priests' lifeway and therefore treat
Mike's illness. Ceremony concentrates many individuals' thoughts
on the performance of a single, communal activity, and this connection, this thong, makes a people out of individuals.

In fact, the process is similar to that experienced by Archilde the
night of the feast. McNickle clearly makes participation in ceremony
and/or verbal arts the crucial ties through which one shares in both
past acts and present actions and thus finds a sense of identity.
Participative acts provide the power to counter potentially destructive influences such as the illness of fear. The cultural core continues
and cultures survive, even if they at first appear dead, and in Mc-
Nickle's presentation of the Dance, one can see the author's concern
for the secret strengths of Native societies that are so easily missed by
the untrained eye.[20] McNickle's vision comes to life to help the
reader discriminate between popular illusion and reality. It is Independence Day at last, for the event provides a cure—through independence from the priests' power—for many other characters be-
sides Mike.

The Dance, like the feast, marks a turning point in Catharine's
story and the story of her people.[21] Catharine's winter has been
difficult, but from it comes a course of action and, like Old Man in
the story of the iron ax, the way is given in a dream. The dream
resurrects the peoples' ancient awareness of, and alignment with,
primal forces. Likewise, Catharine comes to her knowledge in the
old way—after fast and prayer. In her dream, she dies and goes to
heaven, and it is everything the priests say it is. The streets are gold
and the people are at ease; but, as she travels through it, she finds
that it lacks all the things that give the Salish world meaning. The
streams are devoid of fish and there are no animals to hunt—so
there is nothing for the Indians to do. The place is purely spiritual; it
lacks the physical, material lifeways that define Salish identity and
are inseparable from their spirituality. It is understandable that there
are no Indians here either. God sends for her because she is not
happy, and he tells her of the Indian heaven that coexists with his.

When she travels to it, she finds all the things that are good. The people are gathered around their fires, cooking meat and talking. Although she is not allowed to enter because she is a Christian, she is given an option: she can return to life and renounce her baptism.

McNickle, following the four-step framework from Salish verbal arts, has her dream the same dream three nights, and then relive it a fourth when, the night before the Dance, she tells her dream to a gathering of Salish elders that includes Modeste. She has come to them because she wants to be whipped in accordance with an old Salish custom. This act, outlawed by the priests, "will cover the fault," the error of her baptism. To calm their fears of the priests' rules, she states an attitude strongly suggestive of those found in the Salish literary canon: Being in trouble "will be nothing new. We have had trouble no matter what we do and we ought just to forget about it and live as best it seems" (210). Be flexible. Have faith in sources of knowledge, such as dream and communal debate, which have worked before to resolve troubles. Her life as "Faithful Catharine" is at an end. Her whipping expiates the initial event that gave the priests their power—her baptism—and takes the Salish back to an old lifeway. Her heart now light, she sleeps peacefully, without dreaming, because her path to heaven is open once again.

One of McNickle's ethnographic sources, Barbeau's *Indian Days*, contains the ancestor of Catharine's dream. Barbeau credits De Smet's journals for the story and carefully notes the priest's estimation of the Cree man who told it to him: "an adroit impostor who has been baptized."[22] Since it satirizes Christian belief, he discredits the teller, and Barbeau concludes that the Cree man found heaven "too exclusive a Kingdom for the dusky people of the prairies and the mountains." Unlike the other narratives borrowed from collections, this "Cree impostor's" dream is almost exactly reproduced in *The Surrounded*, and one can see what attraction it held for McNickle. For one thing, it comes from his own people, the Cree, but also, in the final sentence of the story, the teller attaches a moral that could be applied to McNickle's own book: "The old-time ways are the only ones that can make us [the Cree] worthy of the wonderful plains in spirit-land, where the numberless herds of buffalo roam day and night for the everlasting happiness of Indian souls."[23] The connection between "old-time ways" and Indian souls is implied throughout the novel, but it is given its clearest expression and demonstration in the Dance.

Archilde is not aware of his mother's renunciation of the priests and their teachings, yet the young man's sometimes "objective" observations at the Dance reveal the change that has taken place because of her dream. In this way, this significant event is structured very much like the evening of the feast. Archilde—once again the observer, then the participant—teeters on the line between two reactions to what is taking place. Before going to the dance grounds, he visits Modeste's tepee and then his mother's. Although he senses the ceremonial quality in the actions of the people, he views them from a distance that is at once respectful and tentative. Archilde's dual background makes him the perfect character for a pivotal point of view; he is one of McNickle's devices for demonstrating both the Anglo and Salish perceptions simultaneously, just as the narrator's description of St. Xavier provides two perceptions of place. When Archilde watches Modeste's thoughtful repose, he equates it with that of a priest preparing for a service, yet he sees the markings being painted on Mike as merely the fancy of the old woman who paints them. For him, they are devoid of meaning, but not for the Salish who create them.

McNickle's use of the mixed-ancestry protagonist deserves some elaboration at this point. It was hardly new. After all, Mourning Dove (Hum-Ishu-Ma) had used it as early as 1913 in her manuscript of *Cogewea: The Half-Blood.* Unfortunately, in her case the ability of the protagonist to provide consistent, profound, and compelling insights into tribal culture was continuously thwarted by the co-author, by the intrusive voice of McWhorter.[24] On the other hand, Archilde bumbles through his confusion producing valuable observations, building patterns, and drawing relationships that allow McNickle to clarify, analyze, and generate perception. Archilde does not proselytize; he discovers.

As an observer, Archilde sees things as someone not conversant in Salish culture would see them; the types of analogies he draws and the beliefs they represent are very familiar to us, for they derive from a comparative approach we employ ourselves when trying to understanding something "new" to our experience. Unfortunately, this reaction often reinforces the popular assumption that Native cultures can only be defined in terms of, and understood in relationship to, symbols central to the beliefs of the dominant culture. This assumption dictated approaches to written narrative, as in sections of *Cogewea*, but also other very popular works of the time, thus catering to their audience's perception of Native cultures and perpetuating the romantic stereotypes McNickle wished to dispel. Oliver La Farge's *Laughing Boy* (1929) is one example. La Farge was not a tribal person; thus, his romanticized approach to explaining Navajo culture in familiar terms, rather than revealing/generating the intricacies of their world view, is understandable, if not acceptable. He was an outsider. Several tribal artists have called attention to the shortcomings of his efforts, but McNickle's comments are germane here: "the text of *Laughing Boy* is clearly that of an outsider looking in from a defined social position upon an alien world. . . ."[25]

Wah'Kon-Tah: The Osage and the White Man's Road (1932) is another example. It was published while McNickle was revising his novel, and he must have been aware of it. Although its author, John Joseph Mathews, was himself an Osage, he chose to present his narrative from the point of view of an Anglo Indian agent. This device allowed him to examine tribal people from the perspective of a character who, supposedly, shared his audience's beliefs and cultural orientation but who was sympathetic to the Indians. The aim was to add credibility, perhaps pathos, to the insights into tribal culture voiced by the agent. Mathews also seemed compelled to compare his Osage characters to those of classical Greece and Rome, to give them "validity" no doubt. The need to reach an audience often led to means that were successful, as in the case of La Farge, yet they did not intimately, accurately, or adequately convey the character of the culture addressed. They do not rely on verbal narrative devices or motifs born of the culture but instead upon written conventions.

McNickle's fiction suggests his awareness of both approaches and their shortcomings. Like Mathews, he, too, wrote a novel that used an Indian agent's point of view, but not exclusively. Chapter by chapter in *Wind From an Enemy Sky*, that point of view is juxtaposed with the perception he wished to evolve—the tribal. His works have an overriding emphasis on tribal interpretations of events; they are Indian narratives. In *The Surrounded*, McNickle's mixed-ancestry

Archilde becomes an even more interesting and innovative device. At first he too seems limited by the fatalistic misconception of the doomed Indian that permeates the popular literature of the time, but he is also actively engaged in a reinitiation into tribal life. This builds a tension between a popular stereotype and evidence that it is baseless, and this tension takes the reader far beyond the conventional "clash between two civilizations" that was the basis of most popular fiction about Native peoples in McNickle's time and since. Like Grepilloux at the first meeting of priest and Salish, Archilde sees the preparations for the Dance through a narrow, Anglo perspective. Then, McNickle immediately plunges his readers into a Salish perception of events by bringing Archilde slowly back to the insights he accomplished at the feast.

When Archilde goes to his mother's lodge where she is preparing Narcisse, he feels once again the affinity for the people he felt so strongly after the stories at the feast:

> Watching her, Archilde felt suddenly happy. She was pleased with her duties in the way that an old art or an old way of life, long disused, can please the hand and the heart returning to it. She took the folded garments out of beaded buckskin and placed them on her grandchild in a kind of devotional act that derived satisfaction from minute observances; in a matter so simple, the least part has its significance or it is all meaningless. (215)

This idea of minute observances, of detailed and deliberate and consequential motions, is at the center of McNickle's interpretation of the lifeway that persists in tribal cultures today. It is the heart of his vision, and he reaffirms its compelling power in his description of Catharine and the Salish using the knowledge of correct action and form to recapture a power lost sixty years earlier.

The "least part" goes a very long way toward explaining the whole—the lifeways of the Salish. Sharing the same movements emphasizes and reenforces shared perception, and it is a thing of hand and heart greatly removed from Western intellect and reason, as depicted in the book. The sense of sharing permeates the celebration as the drum beats to prepare the people. McNickle equates the drum's effect with that of a common heart, "as if the earth had begun to pulse. It was a sound to quicken the blood" (212). Nevertheless, Archilde's flash of insight in his mother's lodge is shaken when he goes to the dance grounds; there, he becomes the outsider again as he watches the white audience's behavior and allows it to sway his perspective of the Dance and of his people.

He finds a circus atmosphere, rather than the solemnity he expects. The Dance is open to spectators, and so draws the people who usually gather to view what they consider spectacles staged for their benefit. Booths sell soda pop and Kewpie dolls to the townspeople, and, as he stands in the crowd of onlookers, Archilde cannot help but feel hurt and ashamed by their lack of understanding and respect. They even jeer an old man as he dances. The Indians are surrounded once again. However, this scene is like all the best in McNickle's fiction; it holds the potential for two interpretations, two reactions. When McNickle spoke to the Missouri State Archaeological Society, he stated that the government's attempts to suppress Indian ceremonialism have been ineffective. Ceremonial activity has simply gone "underground." In the novel, this perspective is the one he gives his readers with the shift of Archilde from the Anglo observer to the Salish celebrant.

Readers may accept Archilde's initial reaction and condemn the insensitivity of the crowd and, by implication, white society, but they must also recognize the implied "inside," the Salish point of view that is McNickle's ultimate concern. As Archilde watches Mike dance, his shame falls away through an act of imagination that joins him once again with the actions of his people. They are physically surrounded, but the dancers are not without power, "a detached element of rhythm, moving unhindered through space."

> For a moment he [Archilde] felt everything Mike felt—the rhythmic movement, the boy's delight in a sinuous thrusting of legs and arms, the wild music of the drum and dancing bells, and best of all, the majesty of the dancers. It really seemed, for a moment, as if they were unconquerable and as if they might move the world were they to set their strength to it. They made one think of a wild stallion running free—no one could approach him, no one would ever break his spirit. (218)

The fact that he feels his people's movement is important. Like his mother as she prepares Narcisse for the dance, he must match his movement of hands and heart to their ceremonial observances—both mundane and sacred—if his feelings are to be more than momentary and solely intellectual. He must find his *somesh*, which will tell him how to act, how to move effectively with his people and within their landscape. As the dancers share their dance, they move beyond the concerns of the present and the resentment that entangle Archilde. They move beyond the response of the insensitive crowd. Only Archilde is hurt by the attitudes the crowd exhibits. The old dancer may be scorned, but his "face showed his inner contentment and he was oblivious of the laughter at his expense" (219). At this point in his education, Archilde cannot recognize that the Salish are indeed moving the world as they test their strength in the Dance. They are removing the power of the priests.

That night, after the spectators are gone, he feels the Salish move in his blood again. As before, he goes from the detached observer to the active participant. His activity is not physical but emotional, as he listens to the men ride their horses around the camp to tell their stories to the people. Their horses' bells make a sound McNickle renders as *"ca-ring, ca-ring, ca-ring,"* and this sound and its implications become integral parts of Archilde's reactions as he sits near his mother's fire. Moreover, he recognizes the change in her and decides not to disturb her contentment. "Her hands had taken her far back into the past that day and he would not drag her forth again" (221). This scene, with its nostalgic suggestion of precolonial times, is an interesting revision of the early draft where the savage Salish sat huddled about a weak fire waiting for the hand of fate to fall:

> She [Catharine] stirred the fire and he watched the sparks fly upward, alive, then dead. They lived just long enough to know. A man's life was too long by comparison. It dragged out his misery, or if he had happiness that too was dragged out until it turned to misery. And he didn't die until he had tasted all of it. One just had to go on, taking everything that came, somehow. . . .
>
> *Ca-ring, ca-ring, ca-ring.* . . .
>
> "My people! Listen to my words! When I was young. . . ." (221)

Obviously, the scene is similar to the dream in "The Hungry Generations." Archilde hunkers near the fire waiting for the hand of fate (Sheriff Quigley) to fall, but in his continued reflection, there is hope. His education progresses. The day's event has cured two generations of Salish—those of Catharine and Mike—and it has taken a third, Archilde's, a long way toward health. Although initially personal and pessimistic, his thoughts finally reveal an inherent ray of determinism. The means of endurance are present in the knowledge of the world's mutability and in a reliance on one's ability to react to changing circumstance by maintaining a feeling and responsive relationship with one's people.

The last sentences of the passage reveal just how close he has come to them. He "sat quietly and felt those people move in his blood. There in his mother's tepee he had found unaccountable security. It was all quite near, quite a part of him; it was his necessity, for the first time" (222). McNickle tells Archilde's story in terms of a journey, an educational quest or process that charts the young man's movement from isolation to integration, and his evolution of a philosophy of life that, like his people's, recognizes the ever-changing nature of the world. But philosophies become real through behavior. Unlike his mother, Archilde does not know how to act. Although her body has not moved in the old ways for quite some time, she remembers what to do, as Archilde sees when she prepares Narcisse for the Dance. He, too, must learn how to behave, to act appropriately by moving in ways that will reflect his Salish nature and help him survive ill fortune and direct his future.

At one point, he tries to help an old Salish woman who is returning from the slaughterhouse with a tub full of entrails for food. He gives her money, when she needs food. Rather than help her, he has confused her with the useless bills. On a lonely ride into the Badlands, he tries to help an old mare—and hounds her to death instead. He should remember his own stallion metaphor for the Salish dancers who, he recognized earlier, possess a free spirit that can never be broken. Like the Salish, the mare wants to be left alone. But Archilde looks at the horse through the eyes of the newcomers to the valley of Sniel-emen. Just as they see the squalor of Indiantown and homesteads as indicative of a Salish character flaw, he takes the mare's appearance as proof of her need for a beneficent remolding. He reacts out of ignorance, just as the people in the story of Spokani when they first shun him because he is too perfect and then attack him because they see him as disfigured by the frog on his cheek (perhaps an interesting parallel to the Noble Savage/Blood-thirsty Savage dichotomy). He rides the mare down, and although her body gives out, her spirit remains unbroken. Archilde recognizes the effects of such a haughty perspective of the world: "She groaned aloud, a final note of reproach for the ears of the man who had taken it upon himself to improve her condition" (242). Each of his attempts reflects an action more appropriate for Max's world than for the Salish, and the results are always damaging. Like Father Grepilloux's, Archilde's actions, born of good intentions, bring ill effects. However, as in the verbal arts, a character has gone off alone and returned with a valuable lesson. But it is not until the fourth, and final, complex event in the story of his education that McNickle shows Archilde making connections that provide him with the knowledge necessary to begin to act correctly.

Catharine's death is hardly unexpected. When she tells of her dream the night before the Dance, it becomes clear that her time may be near. In fact, McNickle's presentation of her death relies heavily upon the reader's memory of certain elements of her dream, elements that now become infused with meaning and significance.

Another change is taking place in the Salish world. Upon entering the darkened kitchen where his mother lies, Archilde instinctively recognizes that change. He looks to the sole source of light, the window. It looks westward, the direction taken by the dead in the Salish mythos, but it is blocked by the crossed bars of the window frame. Immediately, he thinks of Modeste's story at the feast, of "the new thing"—the priests' *somesh*—and a scene that could have become greatly symbolic of restrictions to, and a subsequent loss of, Salish culture becomes instead an affirmation of it by his spontaneous evocation of a story. The oral literature is at work in his world doing what it has always done, providing knowledge by defining relationships and showing how to act: "Here it [the cross] was, staring meaninglessly at him" (257). Its power gone, Archilde can move into action. "He did not want to open his eyes to this strange event," but open them he does, and McNickle's description of his capabilities is pointed: "As he went to fetch the lamp from the adjoining room his moving body was like a strong candle burning in the dark. He knew what to do, how to make use of his wits; that was a wonderful thing" (258). No longer a mere observer but an active participant, he moves and takes control, like Catharine herself the night before, and in preparation for, the Dance. He has a course of action, and like Sinchlep in the story of "The Ram's Horn Tree," he can use his wits. He brings light into the darkness and sees to his mother whom Agnes, his sister, has given up for dead.

There is another interesting but subtle quality to the passage describing Archilde's return from the mountains to his mother's deathbed. If readers reconstruct the series of events immediately leading to it, they will find that Catharine's actions closely suggest the steps described to her in her dream. Agnes tells Archilde that Catharine has remained motionless for hours. In fact, when he arrives Agnes is dumbfounded when her mother revives and says simply, "No priest!" McNickle plays the readers' knowledge of Catharine's dream against the "reality" of the event as it unfolds. As in her dream, she has died and then come back to life to renounce her baptism. There is an implied connection, the remote possibility that Catharine has indeed seen into her own future and learned what is to transpire when she dies. (One wonders what De Smet and Barbeau might have thought of this reaffirmation of a story told by the Cree "impostor who has been baptized.")

The sight of his mother has a profound effect on Archilde. As he nears her bed, his thoughts mark the distance he has journeyed—the term McNickle applies to his growth—in the last year. No longer the outsider, his life meshes with the life of the Salish:

He knelt at his mother's head, thinking as he did so of the night in her tepee on Fourth of July night. The sparks flew up, expired, and he had wished that a person might find oblivion as easily. It was a different matter now. People grew into each other, became intertwined, and life was no mere matter of existence, no mere flash of time. The time that was consumed in moving one's feet along the earth, in learning the smell of coming snow, and in enduring hunger and fear and the loss of pride; all that made a difference. And a still greater difference was this entangling of lives. People grew together like creeping vines. The root of beginning was hard to find in the many that had come together and spread their foliage in one mass. (258)

His journey is nearly complete, and the steps are clearly restated: the feast and Dance provided the basis for his knowledge of how to endure. Also, he sees that life is more than a "mere matter of existence," which implies the potential for self-determination. Likewise, his own experiences have shown him poignant examples of endurance despite travail: hunger in the old woman near the slaughterhouse, fear in all the Salish from Running Wolf to Mike, and the loss of pride in himself when he kills the Badlands mare. These are not beings who bow their heads to adversity and fight when the "hand of the spirit pushed them forward."[26]

Catharine rejects the last rites of the church, and Archilde, who has not yet learned of his mother's dream and whipping, reacts inappropriately by assuming his mother is delirious and that she actually wants him to summon the fathers. The fact that Catharine makes her request in English—a language she has not used in years—should alert her son to the fact that she is addressing him in the tongue he understands best so that there can be no confusion about her desire. He acts too hastily; he drives to the mission while the old woman revives enough to clarify her request. She has denied the priests, but he requires this last bit of knowledge before he can act correctly, in old ways recently resurrected by the Salish. He has yet to recognize that he is not alone, isolated, in his rejection of them.

When he rides to tell Modeste of Catharine's condition and learns of her renunciation of the priests, this last spark, this last flash of insight, completes his education. He has come to the end of a personal quest for a single vision—rather than the schizophrenic stasis generated by the conflict between two backgrounds—and found the communal vision of his people as they return, unnoticed, to a lifeway long thought dead by "the newcomers." He shares in the Salish journey now, and even though he sent for a priest earlier in his ignorance of his mother's change of heart, he realizes that it does not matter since the priests' influence is gone. Only their limited ability to recognize change keeps them "from understanding that the power of the two sticks, the *Somesh* which Father Grepilloux had carried over the mountains, was dissolved. . . . It was unnecessary. *The whip had covered the fault*" (274).

He knows how to act also; he knows what to do. As his people come to share Catharine's passing, he sees to their needs: "Never had he felt so near to these people as now, when he could do something for them. It was a small thing, but it was the first" (269). He accepts the responsibility of kinship by calling for the customary gathering of his people and feeding his kinsmen when they arrive. He does not offer them abstract benefits such as the money he gave the old woman earlier, or the reasoning with which he tried to cure Mike, but instead sees to their practical needs personally, as he should. It may be a small matter, but, as McNickle notes earlier as Archilde watches his mother the day of the Dance, the smallest thing has its significance or else everything becomes meaningless.

Catharine's death and the events that follow it seem to lead to a pessimistic conclusion. It is indeed tragic and symbolic of the history of relations between the Salish and the European settlers, but is it the Armageddon for the Salish that most critics would have us believe? Is it fatalistic? McNickle's purpose could be viewed in the simple terms espoused by Charles Larson:

> The pessimistic ending of the novel, the image of death closing in on Archilde and Elise, is consistent with the backlash against Christianity and the violent events described earlier in the narrative. . . . The future will only bring further impingements from the white man's world upon the Indians of the valley of Sniel-emen.[27]

This is true to a point. Unfortunately, Larson is not alone in his interpretation, for others, such as Louis Owens, still read the novel as a statement of the irresolvable conflict between white and red.[28] The tendency is to focus on the murder-arrest plot and therefore to dwell upon the seemingly fatalistic, classically tragic message it contains. Such views do not address McNickle's major concern, for they disregard a plot, or sequence of events, that takes the novel beyond a simple bleak account of the dispossession of Indians, beyond the obvious and conventional protest novel.

McNickle's purpose in the final scenes of the novel *is* confusing, but these scenes are crafted, as all of McNickle's fiction is crafted, to hold the potential for two conflicting interpretations. The confusion derives from the fact that Archilde is ultimately apprehended for his part in the deaths of Warden Smith and Sheriff Quigley. Signs provided by McNickle, however, direct the readers' attention to another way of considering the happenings of the final pages.

First, we have the long progression of the Salish plot that he has carefully constructed along traditional lines to point the way. It begins with a state of affairs that requires action, then charts the steps to knowledge for Catharine and Archilde, whose resolutions in turn are meant to depict the course of future actions by the Salish. The way of the priests is a failure. They both renounce the priests and their world view. They are thus absolved of the need to act in ways dictated by Euramerican society, for they have returned to correct a course of action from long ago. Moreover, Archilde's actions are almost exactly the inverse of those at the opening of the narrative. There, Archilde was going to leave forever the land of his people and journey outward to blend into the white world that surrounds the reservation; he was going to assimilate. By book's end, he has become intricately enmeshed in the life of his people. He travels into the mountains along the same trails as his ancestors and sees his surroundings much as they had. He makes no effort to return. The interpersonal ties of the tribe supersede the impersonal relationships off the reservation. From the townspeople's point of view, he is an Indian "gone bad" and following in the footsteps of his criminal brothers; from the Salish point of view, he is a redeemed tribal member, an "Indian going good."

Since McNickle is writing for an audience that has its own set of conventions and traditions, the plot emerging from Smith's death must find completion. A confrontation is due; when it occurs, it brings to mind the earlier confrontation, also in the mountains, between Smith and Catharine's family. Again, McNickle inverts the actions to denote Archilde's changed character and the readers' altered awareness of Salish character and culture. Earlier, Louis was killed with a gun; now, the gun is turned on Quigley, the epitome of the Indian hunter and hater. His type brought the gun to the valley in the first place and, as Modeste tells us, changed forever the Salish world. Perhaps his death is a form of poetic justice. At the very least, it marks another transformation in the land of the Salish, the end of another era.

Moreover, in the earlier scene Archilde is completely removed from the event. He is shocked into inactivity by Smith's shot, and, when he awakes from his stupor, he catches only the final result of Catharine's intuitive, natural reaction to her son's death as she sinks her hatchet in the warden's brain. In the final confrontation, Archilde is fully aware of every movement as Elise prepares to kill the old sheriff, but he makes no move to stop her: "What was she up to? Something. Archilde sensed it. He wanted to stop her. He could have reached out his hand and held her back. He stood motionless, seeming to hold his breath" (294). It seems paradoxical, but he takes action by not acting; sometimes, holding action in abeyance can be as important as action itself. Much like the old man in the story of "The Thing to Make Life Easy," he waits. Also, the sense of dread he felt at the first meeting with Quigley in the mountains before Louis's death and the fear he felt after Smith's death are quickly controlled. After Elise fires, Archilde holds her; she has acted to keep them together and the simplicity of her logic captures him. "Frown as he would, hold himself aloof as he tried, still he could not be angry with her" (295). If McNickle's signs are followed, the reader must smile with them, even though a man, an officer of law and order, lies dead at their feet.

When Parker steps from the darkness to arrest them, one sees, and understands, the simple and responsive recognition of yet another change of fortune in Archilde's raising his hands to be shackled. Ironically, he is, in a way, matching the movements of his hands and heart to those of his people, who have long been the prisoners of the newcomers yet have maintained their own freedom of character. Although shackled and with his bodily movements restricted, Archilde is still freer than he was in Portland under the restrictions and constrictions of his host society. Now he is more than an individual, alone and unimportant. His future is intricately tied to his people's, and in this sense of belonging there is an energy that may impel individuals, direct their motions, and help them produce satisfying results. This power is unrealized in the happy ending of the original manuscript.

The events described in *The Surrounded* begin with a conscious choice by Archilde's grandfather and his advisers to send for the priests, and they end with a return to lifeways present at the moment of the decision. The conclusion is not a conclusion, and it is not as bleak as one would assume. Inherent in Archilde's raising of his hands is the resurrection of traditional Salish identity and communal authority, ironic (once again) as it seems. Things have changed drastically since the opening of the narrative, but people like Agent Parker are blind to that change. When he arrests Elise and Archilde, he voices his interpretation of the reality of Salish life in this century: they "can't run away" (297).

It is a view that perhaps the readers shared at the opening of the novel, but now they should see what Parker cannot. The Salish *have* run away. As Modeste tells us earlier, the future resides in his grandchildren. Like all the Salish characters in the novel, they too have renounced the teachings of the priests and returned to earlier traditions and ceremonial practices. Mike and Narcisse, who have joined Elise and Archilde in their flight, escape into the night. They will not attend the mission school again. Instead, they will tell the story of their uncle and his mother and how the two faced the fury of the white world. As Archilde comments earlier, they will survive (273). The Salish may be surrounded in Parker's sense of the word, just as they were at the Dance, but their movements are no longer dictated and restricted by the Church and the lifeway it represents. That the direction they are taking is incomprehensible to people like Parker may save them and ensure their future, just as Indiantown's "lack" of a plan saved it.

Interestingly, McNickle does not finish Archilde's story; he merely stops "talking" to us: *Ies choopminzin. The Surrounded* demonstrates a reaffirmation of traditional ways to gain and employ—through verbal arts and ceremony—the knowledge necessary to act and react. McNickle asserts the efficacy of old ways in modern times, and he was satisfied with the final product, as his correspondence of the time records. Constance Skinner, who read the book in manuscript, wrote of it in glowing terms. McNickle's agent, Ruth Rae, took pleasure in sending him clippings that were highly complimentary; she also wanted to negotiate with movie studios in the hope of seeing it on screen in color.[29] Moreover, within two months of its publication McNickle began receiving responses from acquaintances in Montana. A man named Dusenberry wrote in late March to praise the veracity of the book; he notes the locations of scenes in it and the stories it tells: "You have recalled the stories heard when you were younger. . . ."[30] And in a June letter that must have been even more pleasing to McNickle, Dusenberry reported the reactions of Father Toelman, the local priest, who thought McNickle had "gone completely mad."[31]

Despite its strengths, the book was a crushing financial failure. On the first of August 1936, McNickle received a royalty check from Dodd and Mead; after deductions for small advances and his agent's commission, which amounted to $.93, McNickle got $8.33.[32] Needless to say, the book was not selling, and the publishers decided to let it die a graceful death.

The reasons for its demise are difficult to judge, but clues can be found in early reviews. Mary Heaton Vorse of *The New Republic* emphasized the destruction she found in the book, in particular Archilde's:

> The story of how this destruction takes place progresses with the in-
> evitability of a Greek tragedy. But the book is graver and deeper than
> the story of Archilde. . . . With economy and yet adequately Mr.
> McNickle shows the destruction of a powerful race, conscious that
> they have lost their power, reaching out again to try and reestablish
> it, but always inevitably failing in the face of white encroachment.[33]

To her credit, she notes the fact that this is "one of the few Indian novels where the Indian has not been treated with sentimental-ity. . . ." Florence Milner, in *The Boston Transcript*, focused on the scenery and, like Vorse, the Anglo plot. For her, the stories the night of the feast "are introduced more for preserving a bit of folklore than as a moving part of the story, which is often held up by the tell-ing."[34] But episodes in the book are called "brilliant beads." Such mixed reviews suggest the reactions, and the limitations, of the general audience in 1936.

However, even the informed audience faced the same challenges. Oliver La Farge also reviewed *The Surrounded*, and his remarks are telling. He notes the necessity for writers like Mathews and Mc-Nickle, who "partook of the life they describe," but then gives his own sense of that life:

The modern Indian is, paradoxically, a very decent specimen of
humanity, the possessor of a priceless and beautiful inheritance, a
canker on society, and a fine source of drunkards and prostitutes.
One of the most interesting things about studying him is the manner in which the white race reveals itself in contact with him. His
situation is that of a small group trying blindly to restore a shattered life in an enormous and thoroughly hostile world. . . .

Perhaps the most interesting aspect of Mr. McNickle's book is his
success in catching the whole in small compass, by the exercise of a
thoroughly artistic selection, and writing of such sort that the
reader is primarily interested in an excellent story as such, and only
secondarily in the background, which he gets in proper balance.[35]

The Noble Savage/savage dichotomy is apparent, as it is in La
Farge's own novel, and so is the comparative paradigm. He is interested in "specimens" with which to examine the "white race"
through juxtaposition, and that desire shows through his work as
McNickle, Silko, Hobson, and others have demonstrated. Moreover,
he does not recognize—or else studiously avoids—a resolution to
the social problems he notes. Although sensitive to the power of
McNickle's writing, he does not see the novel for what it is: the first
of a new breed. Which "story," one wonders, did La Farge find
"excellent"?

McNickle recognized the differences between cultural perceptions of story, and in particular narrative as history, as he demonstrates with the histories of the priests' arrival in *The Surrounded*.
This recognition guided his efforts, and a few years before his death
he reiterated his beliefs in a letter to a colleague at the University of
Saskatchewan, Richard Pope:

Conventional historiography as developed in the West is concerned with the grand design; it depicts man's progress through
time in terms of crisis and resolution, great epochs, great moments,
great individual heroes; a kind of diachronic rhapsody. . . .

Indian storytelling presents a contrasting view of man's role in
historical process; the coyote tales are especially good for this.
Coyote is rarely a hero, or if he starts out to be a hero invariably he
ends up a scoundrel or he finds himself outsmarted. There are no
mounting crises, no gratifying denouements. Life is an arrangement

of reciprocal expectations and obligations, and no one is allowed to set himself up as a power unto himself.[36]

This sense of narrative as history was lost on his audience in 1936, and the lack of a grand denouement probably helped *The Surrounded* slip quietly into obscurity.

Fortunately, despite its early demise, the book was resurrected in the mid-1970s when the University of New Mexico Press acquired the right to reprint it. It has been successful since. The quality of the book was not its downfall; its artistic merits produced the more complimentary sections of early reviews. McNickle was, simply put, decades ahead of his time. It was not until the general public, as well as scholars working in Native cultures and literatures, had progressed forty years that such a subtle work could be appreciated. The view of dynamic, enduring Native cultures it presents could hardly have been popular in the 1930s, a decade of forced assimilation. This era saw the publication of James Truslow Adam's *The Epic of America* (1931) that proffered racial stereotypes as fact and history. Yet in 1936 a publisher of scholarly books, the University of Oklahoma Press, rejected Angie Debo's *And Still the Waters Run*, a history of land frauds against the "Five Civilized Tribes." (Fortunately, it was published four years later by Princeton.) Seen from the 1980s, McNickle's portrayal of the powerful core of Native cultures was indeed insightful, and its message prophetic.

The failure must have weighed heavily on the man who saw the product of years of labor and a vast expansion of his awareness slip quietly into oblivion, but his desire to reach white society with his message was not silenced. By the time of the publication of *The Surrounded* he had already begun another novel. He would never see this one published, and the only other novel he was to have printed in his lifetime would never fulfill his need for expresssion as had this first effort.

3   The Journey to the South

The things McNickle learned through the revisions of his first novel had a profound influence on the direction of his life. No longer was he merely the homeless outsider who must be content simply to observe and comment upon the inequities in Anglo/Indian relations—and hope for the future. Like Archilde in his first novel, he moved from observer to participant. McNickle became an active champion for the sovereignty of Native peoples. Under the direction of the progressive John Collier, the Commissioner of Indian Affairs, he worked to bring reform. He traveled the country talking to tribal people and recording their grievances and needs. Later, in 1944, he helped found the National Congress of American Indians, which became an institution, a powerful lobby for Native peoples' rights. He also founded the American Indian Development Corporation, which was to help produce Native leaders capable of directing a multifaceted attempt to wrest the management of tribal holdings from the federal government and place it where McNickle believed it belonged: with Native peoples themselves. In short, the purpose and strategies of the novelist/storyteller led to and became inseparable from those of the activist and academic.

Although McNickle's efforts concentrated on resolutions to immediate problems, he also worked on long-range plans of education which would alter the public's perception of Native peoples. As a historian, he demanded the accuracy and insight that he had worked so hard to attain in his art. The result can be seen in such works as *They Came Here First*. Published in 1949, this work charts what he considered to be the probable history of humankind on this continent. Interestingly, it begins with a narrative. McNickle takes his readers' imaginations into the distant past as humans began their journey to this land from Asia. He places readers at a point of origins, and then imaginatively tracks his ancestors into the present. His scientific endeavors were guided by a strong faith in the intuitive and subjective, as were his expressions of his insights. On the strength of such works, McNickle became a Professor of Anthropology, helping to found the anthropology department at the University of Saskatchewan, Regina. Appropriately, he returned to the land his people left for fear of their lives after the Riel Rebellion, and he returned to teach. He also became a Fellow of the American Anthropological Association, and, like his early inspiration, William Gates, he became a noted authority on Native cultures and history, one who was asked to read manuscripts for well-known publishers. In 1966, he received an honorary doctorate from the University of Colorado.

Through all the various phases of his career, his purpose and insights remained faithfully consistent, as the titles of a later work attest. What was initially published as *The Indian Tribes of the United States: Survivals and Renewals* in 1962, McNickle altered to *Native American Tribalism: Indian Survivals and Renewals* in 1973. Both titles emphasize the cultural core he saw surviving as early as 1935—the sense of community implicit in the word "tribe" and the active process required of community implied with "tribalism"—and his belief that this core was being renewed in contemporary times, despite appearances. (The latter title also removes the arbitrary and nationalistic United States and implies instead continental proportions.) He worked in diverse areas to bring about the change he saw as necessary for Native survival to continue. He wrote in various areas as well, and for various audiences, but the subject was always the same: endurance.

In the early 1950s, McNickle broadened his educational scheme. With *The Surrounded* he had tried to take his message to an adult audience, but his book did not become popular in a society raised on visions of the dying red man. He needed to find another way to attack this inaccurate and damaging myth, and therefore alter stereotypical images of Indians for the present *and* the future. His solution was to write a novel for adolescents. To accomplish this task, he once again undertook a systematic quest for knowledge.

Runner in the Sun: A Story of Indian Maize

The publication of McNickle's second novel fell almost precisely midway between that of his first and his last. *Runner in the Sun* came out in 1954. Although McNickle wrote it as a novel for adolescents, the process of its creation reflects the seriousness with which he approached his task, and its plot reflects his ability to bring numerous resources and insights to bear in the construction of a poignant statement presented in a relatively simple, straightforward form.

The story is set in the Southwest. By the time of its creation, McNickle had traveled a great deal there in his capacity as a staff member of the Commission on Indian Affairs and had taken an active part in projects for Pueblo and Navajo peoples. Ultimately, he bought a home in Albuquerque. In short, the Native peoples and landscape of the Southwest had captured his interest, and this interest motivated his attempt to understand better their perceptions of themselves, their world, and the relationships between the two. Interestingly, his education in southwestern cultures took the same directions as that of his early years. To gain knowledge, he turned directly to the land and people, studied the written accounts of early anthropologists, and then brought both together in a narrative that relies very heavily on local verbal arts. As Alfonso Ortiz notes in his afterword to a recent edition, *Runner* "is a story about Indians told in an Indian way: that is to say, it resembles a story that is told more than one that is written."[1]

McNickle's papers contain book after book of notes that he painstakingly collected over years of involvement with the peoples of the Southwest. These are interesting not only for their historical content but also for insight into his choice of things to record. He notes the names of the people to whom he speaks, the places where they meet, and the content of their talk: the particulars necessary for the bureaucrat. But he records them with the concern for detail and methodology of an anthropologist field-worker. The notebooks occasionally provide either allusions to or renditions of the traditional, verbal stories he was told that related directly to the nature of the problems his informants wished him to address. One entry provides a synopsis of Hopi history from their emergence, or origin, story to their present conflicts with white society. It is dated June 1, 1950, four years before the publication of *Runner*. To tell the story of their current conditions and needs, they had to tell the older narratives that related directly to the present. The entry on the Hopi contains an interesting, yet brief notation:

1—Source of Power
2—Written vs Tradition
3—Policy vs Tradition[2]

In his study of Native cultures in the Southwest—and indeed everywhere he traveled in this country—he found the same conflict between two opposing systems of order: one Euramerican and one Native American. One culture vests its power in written, standardized documents that dictate policy. The other exercises its power through traditions of spoken words. Policy removes the need for moral reflection; it is inflexible and self-limiting. Tradition requires constant self-analysis and reflection; it is mutable and resilient in its reliance on the immediacy of spoken discourse. Each has its own history, its own ways of perceiving events, and its methods for solving problems. McNickle was a focal point where the two ways met.

In the 1930s, McNickle had played a similar pivotal role; as a storyteller in the written medium of the novel, he felt his voice, and his voice had power to bridge the abyss between cultures. In the 1950s, he once again undertook the education of American society through the agency of the novel. There is, of course, an ironic twist in his choice of audience. As a young boy, he was forced to leave family and friends to attend Chemawa because the government was bent upon the assimilation of the Indians by instilling American values in their young; McNickle's goal in *Runner* is to educate American youth in Native values and to help end attempts to disrupt and supplant Native cultures. Turn about is, after all, fair play, and his novel is very subtle in its manipulation of its young audience, a claim that cannot be made for the Indian boarding schools of McNickle's day. It is also compelling, informative, and perhaps even as formative for his young readers as were his experiences in school where he was given a new culture to examine.

In *Runner*, McNickle is a storyteller speaking to children. Thus, as he tells of the events that take place in the life of Salt, the book's protagonist, he stops to explain those aspects of proto-Pueblo culture and perception needed to enable his readers to understand the significance of those happenings. His knowledge came from his own childhood experiences in tribal cultures and his experiences in the Southwest—from the stories he had been told by its people—but also from research into the works published by ethnographers. McNickle's papers include not only the manuscript of the novel but also notes and an extensive bibliography that include the names and works of such notable ethnographers of the Southwest as Elsie Clews Parsons and Adolf Bandelier. He did his homework, and he combined the information from oral and written sources with his own background to create a narrative that provides valuable insights into Native peoples and into the traditions of verbal arts.

There are several drafts and outlines for McNickle's second novel among his papers. Originally entitled "The Boy Who Stole the Sun," the book's setting and various titles reflect his desire to explore the origins of certain contemporary peoples, as well as their literatures. For this reason, he set the action of the novel in a time long before the influence of the European altered forever the Native Americans' world—and therefore their stories. It was a time when oral narrative was the only connection between past and present actions and the future. He also chose to examine cultures other than his own. This was to be the simple, direct, objective, yet imaginative examination of how people might have lived and acted long ago, a fictional equivalent to *They Came Here First*. In fact, four years later he sets the approximate date for the story when he mentions in another work—*Indians and Other Americans*—that the use of maize, or corn, in the area he describes in *Runner* began 4,000 to 4,500 years ago. Since it is set in antiquity, the novel is not an exploration of one culture's history so much as it is an examination of points of origin for several cultures of the contemporary Southwest that share a long-standing connection with the same landscape and similar yet distinct lifeways. In fact, Salt and his people reflect some very basic cultural attitudes and perceptions shared by several tribal peoples in the Southwest.

The geographical setting for *Runner* is also obscured, despite the fact that McNickle provides a map of the region in his book. The

Village of the White Rocks, the setting for the book, seems to be an imaginative blend of Chaco Canyon and Canyon de Chelly. The former is northwest of present-day Albuquerque, and it is marked as Salt's home on the map. Chaco is a quiet place that seems to appear out of thin air from the mirages of the flat, high plains of the region. At its bottom, a small stream provides enough water to feed the trees and shrubs that line its banks. Against the steep canyon walls, a collection of abandoned pueblos marks the ancient presence of the peoples native to what are now called New Mexico and Arizona. Chaco Canyon was an early home for several of the modern tribal groups who now live in the region, and so was Canyon de Chelly, sixty miles to the west of Chaco. The description McNickle gives of the Village of the White Rocks more closely resembles de Chelly, as does the name of one of the ancient pueblos found there: White House. Because both places figure prominently in the literatures of the region, it seems quite possible that McNickle melded both into the setting of his novel. He was less concerned with one specific culture than he was with points of origins for cultures from the area, as can be seen with Salt's journey. Through it, McNickle's readers come into contact with several distinct, yet related, cultures at a remote point in their histories.[3]

And there was another attempt for a "focused obscurity." As the initial title of the book suggests, "The Boy Who Stole the Sun" was intended to present, in writing, a story closely akin to an oral narrative. Native traditions abound in stories about the theft of the sun and about people who traveled to distant, seemingly unreachable places in order to bring something of value to their people. McNickle returns to the distant past to explore how one such story may have derived from a historical event, from the concerns and actions of real people. A second, tentative title—"Journey Into the Sky"—penned in above the first on one draft echoes this motif, but the fact that McNickle rejected both early titles for the final *Runner in the Sun* says a great deal about his purpose and his methods.[4] As in *The Surrounded*, he wanted to use Native conventions, but here the novel was to follow, almost identically and in its entirety, specific motifs of plot and purpose found in the verbal arts of the region. The original titles evoke the mythical qualities of such stories, titles similar to those given them in ethnographies. For a young audience raised with no knowledge of Native oral literatures, however, the tentative titles would hardly have the power to suggest a specific genre of oral history. At best they imply a fantasy or fairy tale instead. In the image found in the published title, McNickle capsulated the action of Salt's journey. The emphasis is on the journey, a universal motif, not on Salt's relationship to past heroes in Native verbal traditions. The title suggests the great outdoors and an individual, not the communal sentiments with which he was ultimately concerned. But its subtitle also suggests a direct connection between history and narrative, with the archaic "maize" and use of the word "story." As in his first novel, he patiently worked to bring his audience slowly to alter its perception and to recognize the potential for mythic results from individual actions. By book's end, McNickle's young readers have new-found knowledge of oral conventions and the beliefs that they perpetuate and have perpetuated for thousands of years.

Since he did not have to deal, at least overtly, with the modern conflicts and complexities addressed in his first novel, McNickle did not need to employ a dual plot structure to force a crisis of perception in his readers. Instead, he used the character of a boy, the hero Salt, to appeal to and then guide his young Euramerican audience to an unfamiliar point of view. At first, McNickle presents the people of the Village of the White Rocks in terms to which his readers could relate. For example, Salt is rebellious yet unsure of himself, set on displaying his maturity but confused by the longings connected with his approaching manhood. These are the pangs of puberty—and therefore immensely evocative for a juvenile audience. Also, by using the journey motif in conjunction with his protagonist's education as he did in *The Surrounded*, McNickle takes his readers through a maturation process that leads beyond the concerns of one individual. In his travels, Salt evolves from a young, naive, and ineffectual individual to an integrated member of his society whose actions lead to his people's survival. At first Salt is more important than his people, but, as his story progresses, the events of his journey transcend this one character because they chart whole societies in ascendance or decline. Indeed, the events are based on those found in Native mythic literatures, and they fulfill a similar purpose here. From a self-centered person, Salt progresses to a mythic hero as he questions his own role in the future of his people. When McNickle's young audience recognizes Salt's growth into a powerful leader, they must question the connection between his actions and his power, and they must try to comprehend the forces that McNickle implies have affected his maturity.

Salt is an attractive, compelling hero for young readers for many other reasons. Initially, he is the champion of the young against adults, the new against the old. He is a recent initiate into the Turquoise kiva—the ruling clan to which his family has belonged for ages. He is also a young man with great dreams and aspirations. Recognizing the decline in his people's corn crops, he decides to act personally. Defying the tradition of planting corn on the top of the bluffs above the village, he plants a hidden, experimental patch near the stream at the bottom of the canyon. This type of independent, assertive action is heroic in the terms of McNickle's young readers, but it violates tribal tradition. When the corn is discovered and Salt is brought before the men of the kiva to answer for his breach of custom, the readers feel the sting of the injustice. The adults chastise him, and the "badge"—the turquoise medallion—of his kiva membership is revoked. He is once again a child, rather than a man. The fact that his corn has grown better than the corn in the traditional fields is insignificant to the adults of the book but is of immense concern for the readers, as are the chastisement and apparent punishment.

Relying upon western logic, they wonder why the obvious is overlooked. The solution to the problem seems simple; plant the corn near the water. When this solution is subordinated by political, social concerns that seem unrelated to agriculture, the result is a dramatic tension that McNickle uses to engage and direct his readers. He quickly clarifies the nature of the problem and then resolves it, through the events of the book, along lines quite different than those posited by his Euramerican audience. The problem of the corn is not simple, but very complex; it is only one manifestation of a larger, more dangerous problem, and this problem has quickly reached a cusp due to Salt's ill-considered action. In short, McNickle sets his book at a point of transition for Salt's people where, as one sees in Native oral literatures, great consideration and care should be taken to direct the future along acceptable lines.

The political conflict McNickle presents in *Runner* is between two kivas, the hubs of Pueblo ceremonialism, but also between two ways of life. The Turquoise clan has traditionally supplied the leader of the people, but its influence is challenged by the Spider clan and its leader, Dark Dealer. The name is not very subtle, nor is the present chief's—Holy One. McNickle presents the universal conflict between good and evil, and he carefully provides these primal forces with faces and stories and actions. Dark Dealer is portrayed as a pragmatist whose evil is defined in very clear terms. He is self-seeking, an individual who will sacrifice the traditions and lives of his people for his own ends. A Euramerican equivalent would quite possibly be the corrupt politician (most probably a Joseph McCarthy); through graft, intimidation, force, and intrigue, Dark Dealer hopes to become chief. In short, McNickle once again presents a character who is initially quite easy for his audience to recognize—a character whose motivations are understandable in the context of its own society—but he also remains true to the culture he presents by giving Dark Dealer a character equally recognizable in its own literary canon. In the context of the cultures of the Southwest—in particular the Pueblo—Dark Dealer is a witch, for a witch is defined as someone who uses knowledge inappropriately, usually for personal gain.

It is important to note that the evil which Dark Dealer represents can be found represented in nearly all the Native literatures on this continent, the Cree and Salish included. The new way of life McNickle has him offer is based on personal desire and ambition; it is tradition supplanted by an anarchy based upon individuality, the antithesis of order and community and endurance as a people. For a Euramerican audience bred on American literature which usually idealizes individuality and personal aspiration, the roots of Dark Dealer's evil are easily lost in the superficial: his devious and mean actions. The evil of his motivations is not understood until Salt has completed his journey south and the young readers have witnessed the end results for societies that aspire to Dark Dealer's ideals. *Runner*—like *The Surrounded*—defines the strengths of Native American tribalism, and McNickle found ample illustrations of this ideal in his research of oral literatures from the Southwest.

Through the events of the book, McNickle moves his characters from representations of possible history to the probable origins of mythology. In the literatures of the Southwest, one can find many examples of the approach adopted by McNickle. Elsie Clews Parsons records one such story in *The Pueblo of Jemez*, which is representative of others of the region and reflects the subject matter of McNickle's novel. "The Emergence" opens at *wawanatutu*. This is a specific place in the physical landscape of the Pueblo peoples that some translate as "White House," and McNickle's imaginative blend of Chaco Canyon and Canyon de Chelly is strongly reminiscent of it. It is also a place in the mythic landscape of their oral literatures, for it was here that the people of Jemez were transported into a new existence. Here the people used the medicines that Parsons defines as "the 'mothers' (tseesh)" to move out into the contemporary world. Fotease is the man who organizes the move; he calls the people together to explain how things will proceed, just as his ceremonial descendants—the men called Fotease today—continue to do: "Let us see, my people, if our customs and medicines are going to be good, are going to have power. If they have power, we shall live when we come out into the world, we will bring rain and crops and good health. And we will observe our ceremonies."[5] They perform the ceremonies and their power is proven. In a very brief space, Parsons's informant has given the very basic tenets of his people's lives. The ceremonies provide life by bringing rain and crops, and their performance is synonymous with good health. The health and therefore survival of a people are tied directly to actions and events in the physical world, events that they may initiate and direct by coming together to exercise their beliefs and exert their power.

Ceremonies inside the kivas are sacred and private, but once they are completed, the initiating society emerges from its kiva and the whole community shares in the celebration. This pattern of coming together, or convergence, followed by emergence is repeated throughout the year, giving structure to time; it is characteristic of Pueblo ceremonialism, and it therefore plays a major role in the oral stories that provide the basic beliefs of these peoples. Like all Native ceremonial patterns, it provides order and unity for a people through a shared past, a shared language, and shared movement, and these qualities can be found in the origin stories of many pueblos.[6] The survival of the people is contingent upon their ability to tap the power found in communal unity and movement, and this power is McNickle's primary concern both as historical subject and contemporary lesson. This alone allows repeated transcendence and rejuvenation and, as recorded by Parsons in the origin story from Jemez, the continuation of the world.

As "The Emergence" story continues, the people demonstrate their power further; they "dress the sun," or make prayer sticks for the sun. Once again, their actions influence the physical world by working a change of seasons. First, they bring winter, and the society called batash breaks up the frozen ground and brings spring. Then the people make the four sacred mountains that will provide the cardinal points of reference in their new world and, as the storyteller says, all this "was done just as they wanted it, perfectly good."[7] Because their movements have been perfect and the results those desired, the people emerge into the new world. They now have power to direct their future, but they also have new responsibilities. They must continue to perform those actions that ensure health, crops, rain, and the movement of the seasons.

Once out into this world, the founders of Jemez turn southward and their migration is also guided by their sense of responsible action. The people travel in a specific order, and when they stop for the night, the movement of their journey is translated into ceremonial movement. Again, their actions are "done just right," and the desired results achieved. They move perfectly, and this concept of perfect motion is closely related to McNickle's vision as presented in his first novel and explored fully in his last.[8]

In both oral and written stories, characters' movements are the heart of narrative strategy, giving the illusion of plot development or progression. In Native verbal arts—and in McNickle's fiction—these same motions also dramatize, without comment, the continuity between past and present, between an individual and a people. Actions produce the "moral," not the narrator. When Catharine prepares Narcisse for the Dance, McNickle notes the movements, the actions, that speak of her recent reinitiation into the lifeways of her people. By sharing a way of moving, they share an unstated perception of their world. In *Runner*, McNickle uses Salt's journey in a similar way and for a similar end, but he also draws upon the worship of the sun, migration stories, the relationship between health and ceremony, and the pattern of convergence and emergence in his attempt to convey the points of similarity among many of the tribal groups of the Southwest. His characters possess the heroic statures of those found in the verbal traditions he studied, and their concern for appropriate actions reflects the power that has enabled the survival of many other Native peoples in modern times.

The Holy One is one such character, but, despite his stature in the tribe, the ancient, wise elder lives in a cave above the pueblo, isolated from the people he is supposed to lead. At times, he acts quite mad, and the people wonder if he has lost his mind, as well as his power. However, he has knowledge they lack, and his actions are deliberately directed by that knowledge. When he tells Salt why he acts as he does, he clarifies the central conflict of *Runner*:

> "We are captives, you and I. To protect you, they take away your badge. For my own protection, I leap around like a goat. We won't be touched while we are as we are, but it has its disadvantages. It is a game we play while we wait, and you must understand that."
>
> "That is what I don't understand, Grandfather. What do we wait for?"
>
> "For the enemy to show who he is, and how he intends to move."[9]

The Holy One's isolation ensures that he will not be tricked into ill-considered actions. He waits because he knows that the challenge to his authority is a threat to the survival of his people and that it is representative of a still deeper problem. Another force moves Dark Dealer, and this force, which must surface, is what has made the evil one's new way seem attractive to some and a danger to all.

McNickle leads his young readers from one intriguing mystery to another as he moves through the complex strata of the problem faced by the people of the Village of the White Rocks and, if one considers them carefully, problems strikingly similar to those faced by modern peoples, especially those lulled into the complacency of the Eisenhower years. The trouble with the corn, Dark Dealer, and the people's wavering faith are symptoms of stasis. They have ceased to be a dynamic culture; they have quit changing. But a change, in Dark Dealer's terms, is in the wind. It is a tenuous time for the people, a time when actions must be carefully considered in the context of past experience (spoken stories) and current custom (ceremonial practice). It is a time when the forces affecting transitions must be identified and faith in stories and ceremonies re-affirmed. In McNickle's terms, it is a point of primal considerations, when the actions initiated to respond to Dark Dealer's threat could quite possibly result in the crafting of new stories to tell future generations of this time when change came and the people reacted well. And like the people in the Jemez origin story, the people of the village must work together to direct their survival if they are to act well, do perfectly.

As one can see in the oral literatures of McNickle's own experience and his rendering of them in his first novel, constant change or transformation is synonymous with creation and life, and in oral stories it is the foundation for all events. Whether it is the story of "The Thing to Make Life Easy" or of Archilde Leon's reintegration into the lifeways of his people, the events evolve from one basic, cultural given: the world is mutable, and the people can work transformations and thereby direct their own future. This is equally true for the Native cultures of the Southwest. As one can see in the story of "The Emergence," the yearly transformations of the seasons and rains—and therefore of crops and health—are carefully guided through ceremony, but also through the actions of individuals who must be directed by an abiding concern for their people and their world. McNickle saw this sense of duty and responsibility at work as he toured the Southwest and worked with Native peoples, as his notebooks record, and in it he must have recognized his kinship with them. His people—and indeed all Native peoples—share a similar faith in their ability to move the world through shared belief and action. It is, in fact, a sign of self-determination on a continental scale. As McNickle saw, it is the basis for the durability of Native cultures, a durability built over thousands of years and, as *Runner* implies, it has been challenged seriously by the incursion of the European.

But first, the problem must be analyzed. So it is that the Holy One, in his role as elder and storyteller, recounts the history of circumstances leading up to the cusp the people now face. He thereby clarifies the true nature of the problem by placing it in context. Like Modeste in *The Surrounded*, he provides the longer narrative, the "big picture." Long ago, the people lived a contented life, to the south and west, until a nearby volcano erupted, scattering the people to the four winds. Obviously, Sun Father was angry, and no one knew why. They fled into the mountains and canyons to live in caves, hiding from his wrath. Quite literally, their world had crumbled around them, a very radical change. Salt's home is only one isolated village of a once prosperous, unified people, but for a generation they have withdrawn from interactions with other villages. As a result, they are no longer healthy. As the Holy One says:

> "A field of corn is like a village of people. . . . If people stay too long among themselves, they weaken themselves, some families die out entirely. . . . A race of corn will become weak in the same way. . . . Is it a new race of corn that is needed, then? I cannot say. Maybe what is needed is that our people should change." (165)

The world changed. The isolation that resulted, and then crystallized over the years, came from fear and confusion and a questioning of ancient relationships with their world. The message for contemporary Native peoples is subtly implied.

Moreover, as the old one notes, the fate of Salt's people is inextricably tied to that of the drying climate and their Mother Corn, and what the reader might have initially accepted as a quaint deification of a food source becomes something much more complex as this relationship is explicated through McNickle's narrative. Both the corn and the people suffer from the inbreeding caused by their isolation, which was caused, in turn, by their fear. McNickle is quick to point out that nothing lasting is ever constructed out of fear. The people and the corn need to be infused with "new blood," but they must also address the original sense of fear that produced their isolation and must reaffirm their relationship with the forces in their world, like the sun.

Holy One voices the faith and insight one finds in verbal arts in such characters as the old man in the Salish story of the iron ax. They recognize the appropriate time and ways to react and provide the proper perspective on current events. When he is visited by Salt, he tells the young man how things will end:

"You think things out. And so I am sure you will be a great leader
of the people someday. Also that is why I talk to you freely, and
someday may depend on you. But these men [Dark Dealer and his
clan] are not strong enough to win the people over. They will use
fear if they can. They will try to make the people afraid of me, or of
you, or of anyone who is trusted by the people. A few weak ones
will accept fear as a way of action—and out of fear they may use
knives and spill blood. But nothing is built on fear, and they will
pass away." (53)

Given the long history of humanity he possesses through the stories,
he can surmise the ultimate results of current transitions, but he
cannot foresee the specific, immediate actions that will power the
transformations needed to ensure success for his clan. This working
out, or finding, of the correct path to the future will be the result of
one person's efforts, as it is in many Native oral stories where one
character is guided by the knowledge of the past to be gained from
people like the Holy One. It is also, of course, a subtle message for
McNickle's young readers, who face the fears fostered by McCarthy
and the Cold War.

The old man also instructs through his actions. He realizes that if
he remains in the pueblo trying to deal daily with the influences of
Dark Dealer, he will be susceptible to the emotional reactions that
any undisciplined person might experience: "But if I lived down
there, with those lies and secret meetings, I would forget my duty.
. . . I might take my knife or my club and destroy these trouble-
makers" (53). Sometimes the simple, direct approach, usually violent in nature, is far more damaging than the problem it is meant to
correct. Such actions would violate what should be a person's primary concern: the healthy continuation of one's people. The simplistic solutions McNickle's young readers posit at the beginning of
the book prove inadequate, and even dangerous, by subsequent
knowledge. They are left with a complex puzzle, but no immediate,
logical solution to it. Barring such direct action as force, how are the
people to react to Dark Dealer's threat? Once again, McNickle turns
to the verbal arts for an answer to the dilemma he portrays.

How does one learn how to move to counterbalance evil forces
trying to destroy one's culture? In *Runner*, as in *The Surrounded*,

McNickle employs a long-standing tradition. Holy One has a dream as he patiently waits, alone:

> "Three different times I have had a certain dream. Each time a sacred person talks about our village and tells me that our troubles will not be solved by ourselves alone, that we must go outside of ourselves to find help. . . . If a journey must be attempted, it will have to fall on a young man; one who thinks of his people, not of himself; one who will give his life, if necessary, in order to save his people." (54)

In a brief space, McNickle gives his readers a synopsis of countless stories from the Native oral literatures of this continent. A problem arises. A time for change is at hand, and the knowledge of what to do is sought. A "sacred person" intervenes. A quest, a journey, is needed, completed, and then rendered to narrative. Thus, *Runner* explores the possible origins of the contemporary stories of Native peoples; it examines how historical happenings—such as the eruption of a volcano, the effects of isolation and inbreeding, or the distribution of corn over a geographical area—may have been transmitted through the medium of the verbal arts. But it also demonstrates his idea of how the universal struggle between good and evil can be won.

In McNickle's terms, the educational attraction of many heroes from verbal arts lies in their humble births and their refusal to consider themselves extraordinary, exceptional. They are simply people who act in the appropriate ways at important times to help their people when they need it most. Their stories then come to exemplify traits and perceptions that are desirable in the culture they represent. However, appropriate actions are not haphazard. Heroes learn them from numerous, proven sources: from communal reasoning and discussion, from a personal relationship with a power being (whom Holy One calls a sacred person), from a personal quest into the world, and oral literature. *Runner* demonstrates all four through the meeting of the Turquoise Clan, the Holy One's dream, Salt's journey, and the story that tells of it. Salt is selected for one simple reason. Although others may be stronger, only he has the primal requirement: a passionate desire to serve his people. He also possesses innate characteristics that mark him as exceptional in other ways.

Salt has a mysterious, intuitive ability that is highly suggestive of his relationship with primal forces in his world. When the Holy One tells him the story of how his ancestors fled the volcano and the Sun, he reacts immediately, instinctively, and his reaction pleases the old man:

> "Grandfather, I love the Sun, our Father Sun, and I believe we should no longer dwell in caves."
>
> Salt glanced up, and his face felt suddenly hot when he saw how the Holy One smiled at him.
>
> "Perhaps you will be the one to lead them away from here. Perhaps you will return our people to the broad valley and the gleaming waters." (56)

And of course he is the one, because he does not fear a being upon whom his people once depended. However, first his faith and inherent abilities must be honed and disciplined. He must learn how to acquire the knowledge of how to act, and it is the rapid course of events that teaches him:

> In the course of one day's journey of the sun, he had traveled from a boy's concern with the hunting of rabbits to a knowledge of the dangers with which his elders lived. It was a long journey to make in so short a time. His mind had to take it in. His flesh had to find warmth again. He had to learn how to act in a threatening world.
>
> The elders were fond of saying that, if a man expected to find truth, he should seek it alone. Salt was not sure it meant the same thing, but he had discovered that he could think better . . . when he went off by himself. (73)

McNickle describes, through the personal perspective of a young man, the necessity of a traditional vision quest: the desire for knowledge of how to help, the aid of a helper (Sun), and the removal, for a time, from his people. When Salt begins his long journey to The Land of Fable (present-day Mexico), these characteristics not only sustain him but also contribute to his success. These are the qualities of maturity espoused by McNickle in the novel, and by the cultures he examines.

The Holy One tells Salt at their first meeting what a boy must do to become a man and what a man must do to act responsibly. First, he chastises the young boy for not seeing beyond the immediate problem of the water and corn crops, and for considering the people ignorant because they have not done what he thinks is obvious—move the corn fields to the stream. And then the old man marks the path to maturity: "True, I have told you that our people live in darkness. An old man may talk thus if, in addition to his years, he has listened to many, has reflected on what was said, and maybe learned something of the purpose of life" (57). This is the way of Salt's education. On his journey, he hears and sees a great deal, reflects upon the significance of what he experiences, and then— the night of his return—remembers so that he can share his findings with his people.

To initiate Salt's education along these lines, the Holy One challenges him to find the secret passageway from the cornfields to the pueblo, at the threat of his life. By doing this, the old man forces the boy to use his instincts, reason, and innate powers—including an implied relationship with the sun—to solve a puzzle but also to bolster his courage and confidence. This is a dry run that turns the boy into a man adequately prepared to represent his people on the long journey into The Land of Fable. The search for the passage also prepares McNickle's audience. To find the way, Salt must look, literally, below surface appearances, as the readers must if they are to understand that Native peoples and their traditions are not relics of the past but lively forces in the present, which have faced millennia of threats and catastrophes and have survived.

McNickle's most obvious deviation from oral narrative traditions is the brevity with which he handles the journey itself. He does not describe in detail the long trip nor Salt's daily movements because he has already given his audience the models of behavior that such details usually provide in verbal arts. The Holy One has told us how a man should move and how he should learn. McNickle's narrative of the trip, however, follows a traditional framework. It describes four major events on Salt's quest to the south: his stay with his kinsmen to the southwest, with Yucca Flower Woman in Culiacán, with Ocelot near Lake Patzcuaro, and with Tula in Culhuacán. Each event marks both a step backward along the trail of Mother Corn as she came originally to Salt's village and also a new phase in the dawning awareness of a young hero. Also, the farther south he goes, the more he is attracted to the sun, physically as well as metaphorically, as each meeting brings him into contact with a people progressively more materialistic—more wealthy, but further removed from the ideals of human behavior that McNickle wishes to stress.

Gradually, McNickle takes his young audience farther from the cultures of the Native peoples of the Southwest and closer to the materialism of Euramerican society (and his audience) by presenting—either directly or obliquely—the cultures in which European explorers recognized qualities somewhat akin to their own. Ironically, their recognition of shared motivations led them to believe that they had found the pinnacles of Native "civilizations": the Mayan, Aztec, and Toltec. By the time Salt reaches the home of Tula, however, it has become obvious that each culture is increasingly class-structured, increasingly oriented by individuality, and therefore, in Native terms, inflexible and doomed to destruction. These are cultures on the decline, even though they contain individuals like Ocelot and Tula. These two men are innately moral, but they are no match for the social systems that are rapidly gaining control. Sweeping social change is taking place, and Ocelot and Tula are forced to act against their consciences in order to survive personally.

This conflict between the personal and communal echoes the conflict between Dark Dealer and his people, and it marks the disastrous results. In such a system, people become objects, useful as human sacrifices for the good of an elite. These cultures are dying, yet Salt is able to extract from them the things necessary for his own people's survival. He finds the trail to the broad valley of the gleaming waters of which the Holy One spoke earlier. He brings back a new strain of corn, and a girl who will provide his people with new blood. He acquires the knowledge of what they must do, and not do, to survive, for he has seen what can happen to a culture when it adopts the ways exemplified by Dark Dealer. This final bit of knowledge alters his behavior and thus marks his evolution from a boy to an important man: a leader of his people and a legendary figure.

When Salt returns home, he finds that all is as the Holy One foresaw. Dark Dealer's power was short-lived because it was based on fear; the Turquoise Clan once again is in possession of the pueblo. Also, the time spent away from the pueblo has had a profound effect upon Salt, and McNickle explores in great detail the youth's transformation, as well as the transformations of others, in the final pages. As Salt retraces his steps northward bringing with him the young girl Quail, whom he has saved from human sacrifice, he grows stronger: "He was thinner than he should be, but his strength was tireless. He seemed ready to go on forever, searching for whatever it was that his spirit needed" (220). His spirit needs his people and their ensured health, and he is no longer plagued by doubt nor lacking in confidence, despite the fact that he is still not aware of how successful he has been on his quest. When he reaches the village, his acquisition of knowledge, his education, is completed by the events of that evening as he comes once again among his people. As in the verbal tradition, this concentration leads to power and transition into yet another phase of their existence. No longer the carefree youth of the book's opening, no longer an individual acting on his own, he becomes a responsible focal point of his people's energy.

The people are impressed with Salt's traveling companion. On her forehead, Quail bears the brand of a slave, but the people look at its design and see it as the mark of the sun. When Salt begins to correct them, however, he mysteriously stops:

> The words he would have uttered, explaining the slave mark, dissolved and were gone. The mark itself—the little circle, with parallel lines running to the four directions—glowed brightly as the girl stood before the firelight. And the people spoke in wonder. (227)

Throughout the final pages, McNickle makes continuous use of light as a descriptive device that, coupled with repeated references to the sun, imply the presence and influence of Father Sun. This influence, although subtly presented, is reinforced by the changes that take place in the characters themselves.

Quail undergoes a transformation, and the Holy One recognizes the full implication of her coming to them when he watches Salt react to the intervention of Dark Dealer. The troublemaker's clanspeople are starving, and so he comes to ask forgiveness for his clan and permission for them to return to the pueblo. He offers himself in

return. No longer the haughty, self-seeking individual, he too has
undergone a transformation: "All ornaments had been stripped
from his body; he walked barefooted, his only garment a breech-
clout" (228). McNickle offers him in direct contrast to the people of
ancient Mexico; unlike them, he is shorn of his excessive materialism and individuality, as his appearance and actions denote. Seeing
this change, Salt responds quite differently than he, or McNickle's
readers for that matter, would have before his journey. When called
upon to judge Dark Dealer, he thinks of Tula, who selflessly helped
him escape with Quail at the threat of his own life, and then
responds:

> "It is not for us to say whether any man has lived his life well," he
> ventured, and as he spoke his voice grew stronger. "Each man can
> answer only for himself. If Dark Dealer finds in his heart that he
> has not done well, and asks us to take him back, we cannot refuse.
> We cannot deny him his chance to make the gift which will fulfil
> [*sic*] his life. I say, bring them all back, and make our people whole
> again." (229)

Such a judicious response to someone who has worked so much evil
is understandable when one recognizes the change that has come
about in Dark Dealer. He now has his people's best interests at heart
and will willingly sacrifice his own life for theirs. This quality is the
one that launched Salt on his journey; it marks the strength that he
has for his people. It will be doubled by Dark Dealer's return and the
peace and unity it will bring. Contrite, Dark Dealer pours dirt on his
head. "It was the supreme submission" (230).

The people are awed by Salt's actions, except for the Holy One
who sees Salt's decree as the final event in the transition he knew
would come:

> "Power is here. The power to restore peace in a bad heart. The
> very power needed by our people. . . ."
> "If we ask ourselves how this power comes to this boy, I find that
> answer not strange either. Here is this girl, bearing some sign, per-
> haps of the sun, on her brow. Bring her here, where we can look
> upon her. . . ."
> Presently she stood beside Salt; and the people, gazing upon her,

saw the mark upon her brow, and the wide, longing look in her
eyes.

Then they drew closer, as if pulling sheltering walls around her.
(231)

She quite literally brings them closer together, and she is renamed
Red Corn Woman for the direction from which she came. Then
something very interesting happens. When Salt looks at her, he sees
"the slave girl vanish, and beauty stand before him" (232). The
gathering of the people, the reconciliation with Dark Dealer, the
influence of the sun, the experiences of Salt's journey, and the
presence of Quail all come together with Salt's people at this one
point in the narrative, and the result is beauty. McNickle's story
describes how one person may make a difference and may become
much, much more than an individual.

Salt sees his companion transformed, and then he remembers the
seed corn she carries; suddenly, he sees a pattern in his journey and
life. His quest has not been a failure as he feared earlier, but a
success, and it takes these final events to make the pattern complete
and therefore recognizable. Salt's journey ends in the creation of a
new story and ceremony that produce the power to promote health,
and McNickle's narrator caps the story with the people's migration
down from their isolation:

> So they left the Canyon of the White Rocks, which today stands
> tenantless and soundless. They traveled southward, down from the
> mountains, into the valley of the big fields. Land was set aside for
> them by those who were there first, and the new corn, when
> planted and watered abundantly, produced such harvests as had
> never been known. In their rejoicing the people performed a new
> ceremony, which they called Red Corn Dance. In time they built a
> great village of adobe walls, and dug canals to lead water from the
> river to the planted fields.
>
> There they lived in peace and supported one another. (233)

In McNickle's own words and in keeping with the cultures he
depicts, it is completed in "beauty"; the motions have been perfectly
executed.

Like the story of "The Emergence," *Runner* tells of a difficult and formative time in the life of a people. It is a time of confusion and disorder when people step forward to lead, people whose actions in turn become the basis for stories that not only tell what was done but reinforce the basic values and ideals of the culture for present and future generations. Their stories tell of the origins of cere-mony—how they came about, what effects they have, and why they must be performed. Red Corn Woman and Salt—as their names suggest—reflect primal characters in enduring narratives told by contemporary peoples in the Southwest. Although they are rendered through the medium of a written novel, they possess the characteristics of the verbal traditions from which they were born. McNickle's novel more closely resembles contemporary works, like Silko's *Ceremony* (1977), than any of its own generation.

McNickle has posed intriguing questions for his young readers. What if the stories told among Native peoples are more than fic-tional fairy tales? Perhaps they tell of actual happenings and of the qualities of a people that allowed them to endure even though their orderly world fell into chaos and their very survival was threatened. And what if the current material condition of Native peoples is not indicative of their durability as cultures? What if the stories are still being told and people are working toward yet another transforma-tion in a long series of transformations? Will they survive? In short, he works to capture his readers' imaginations, just as storytellers and their oral literatures do, and, of course, to show how Native cultures survive in the present despite the challenges they face.

The publication of *Runner* was indeed timely. The Korean War and World War II were recent history and the atomic bomb a new, threatening reality. This too was a time of transitions, and the values that McNickle presents in his novel run counter to the chaos and alienation of the era, for Anglo and Indian alike. Selfless unity, shared action, and faith are the ideals he saw as the counterbalance to current trends, and these are the ideals he saw as the strengths of Native American patterns of belief. This was also a time when Indian tribes faced one of their most trying tests in modern times, for under the direction of Douglas McKay, the Interior Secretary, the tribal status of many groups was terminated. No longer considered a people by the federal government, these groups had no legal re-course when lands and hunting and fishing rights were taken from them once again, and educational and social programs lost funding as treaties were ignored, "legally." The qualities that had unified tribes, defined their cultures, and therefore provided identity were even more crucial now. McNickle presents these ideals imaginatively in *Runner* just as a traditional storyteller would present them orally. He continued to do so in his third novel, where he further refined his vision and rendered even more clearly how Native peoples move to direct their own futures.

4 A Vision of Movement

Wind from an Enemy Sky

Wind from an Enemy Sky was published in 1978, twenty-four years after *Runner in the Sun* and the year following McNickle's death. At first glance, it appears quite different from his earlier works. In it, McNickle does not focus on the Salish of his own experience, nor does he imaginatively examine historical peoples such as the proto-Pueblo. Instead, he creates a fictional people who act as a pantribal representation of certain qualities of tribalism he wishes to explicate. After all, over the years his concern for his own future came to encompass the futures of all Native cultures on the continent, and from the research and revisions he undertook to portray accurately the cultures in his first novels came the vision he evoked, clarified, and generalized in his last.

In 1976 his publisher, Harper and Row, asked him to complete a form calling for information about the novel's origins and subject, for use in publicity and promotion of the novel. His responses provide a number of interesting insights into its composition:

> The idea for *Wind from an Enemy Sky* was carried around in my head for years. In 1937–38 I had participated in negotiations with the Museum of the American Indian (Heye Foundation) for the return to the Mandan Indians of a sacred (medicine) bundle, which the Museum had obtained in circumstances similar to those described in the story. The present draft of the novel is the last of many versions of the story I attempted over a twenty-year period. I experienced many interruptions in the writing, and each interruption seemed to result in a new approach to the material. . . . About two years ago I returned to the manuscript and rewrote the entire script in about six months.[1]

The final draft reflects nearly forty years of revision. As early as 1940, McNickle began to negotiate for the publication of "The Indian Agent," the original title found on drafts of the novel remaining in his papers at the Newberry. Also, later in the correspondence with Harper and Row, he states the autobiographical nature of his fiction: the "incidents in the novel follow very closely the record of government dealings with the Confederated Salish-Kutenai Indians . . ." and, although *Wind* is not autobiographical per se, "it has its roots in the reservation life I knew as a tribal member. . . ." [2] As always, he draws upon his early years for inspiration and then refines its expression through laborious revision.

For its manuscript history alone, *Wind* is a significant document. Its evolution covers four crucial decades for Native Americans. Beyond this historical significance, the manuscripts resolve any doubt or ambivalence about McNickle's perception of his people, or Native peoples in general, for they reveal the depths to which his lifelong quest for knowledge and understanding took him. McNickle's last novel, and its various incarnations, examines more clearly than any of his other writings the possible existence of a unique relationship between Native peoples and this land. This relationship is recognizable through the ways that his characters move, for it is through motion/action that people and place interact. Their actions produce power and knowledge that allow them to affect their world directly. The relationship is exercised and expressed through ceremony and ritual but also through individual inspiration. McNickle began to examine these connections in the thirties with *The Surrounded*, but his later works attest to his continued interest. As late as the year of his death, he continued to try to express, through the revision of *Wind*, the vision he had been given forty years earlier.

In 1971, McNickle retired from the University of Saskatchewan, but in 1975 he was still actively engaged in the study of history and anthropology as the director of the Newberry Library's Center for the History of the American Indian, a center that now bears his name. He also occasionally read manuscripts submitted to the University of California Press for publication. He read one such manuscript in 1977, only a few months before his death, and the responses to it that he sent to the editor, Alain Henon, mark the duration of the perception of Native peoples that he originally formulated in the thirties. He suggests that the writer of the manuscript take "a longer range view" than the one presented, and then he provides the broader perspective, just as a traditional storyteller might in order to direct the education of a young person:

> The argument here [that McNickle proposes] starts from the prem-
> ise that the Native American race was highly adaptive, as witnessed
> by the extremes of climate and terrain to which the people shaped
> their lives. Not only was the movement through space impressive,
> from end to end of two continents, but the vertical movement
> through time called for critical adjustments during epochs of dis-
> ruption and change. . . . The coming of Europeans in the 16th and
> 17th centuries differed from earlier climatic and environmental
> crises only in that it happened rapidly and allowed aboriginal so-
> ciety but little time to adjust its values and develop the technology
> needed to survive in changing circumstances. After four hundred
> years, a brief span in the history of a race, the native Americans are
> still making adjustments—and surviving.
>
>   This would suggest that the Indians of eastern Canada, like In-
> dians elsewhere, accepted change as a normal process of nature.
> For a people who aspired to live in harmony with nature, the atti-
> tude of acceptance is consistent. . . . To live in harmony with nature
> is to trust nature, in the confidence that good times would always
> follow bad times.[3]

This belief is consistently expressed throughout his fiction by his emphasis on the durability of Native cultures and the maintenance of their cultural cores: ceremonies, social structures, and oral litera-tures. But how do they make the "adjustments" that are necessary? Where do they gain the knowledge of how to direct their future? In *The Surrounded* he outlined the ways to knowledge for the Salish, and in *Runner in the Sun* he created an imaginative rendering of these same paths, set in ancient times, which he found to exist in cultures in the Southwest. In *Wind*, he generalizes these same ways, but also the primal sources of knowledge in the world, sources that are recounted in myth.

   As early as 1940, McNickle began to flirt in his fiction with the "mystical" or metaphysical aspect of Native experience. This seems odd at first, considering his earlier letters to William Gates in which he praised the scholar for his objective, scientific handling of Native materials. However, some cultures may not consider science (as "objective reason" or knowledge derived from experimentation) and mysticism as mutually exclusive concepts or realms of experience. He hints at the conjunction of the two in *The Surrounded* when he describes Running Wolf's disappointment as Father Lamberti refuses the eagle wing because the Jesuit wants only to administer to the Salish "spiritual" concerns, not their temporal affairs. He also suggests the prophetic potential of dream when he has Catharine dream of her own death and later describes her last hours in terms that shadow the events of the dream itself. In *Runner in the Sun*, dream once again conveys the knowledge of what must be done to ensure survival for Salt's people. But in the early manuscripts connected with the composition of *Wind* are found, as nowhere else in McNickle's canon, the unqualified, overt expression of connections between primal forces in the Native world and humankind.

The manuscripts are a Gordian knot. Some pages obviously date from an early draft: numerous page numbers have been crossed out once or twice and replaced by others; some pages are handwritten, others neatly typed; and there is an early outline and synopsis of characters that McNickle prepared for submission to his publisher in the early 1940s. From it Rafferty, the Indian agent, is the only character who remains in the final, published draft. But there is also the manuscript for a short story entitled "Snowfall," and this narrative about the relationship between an agent and a Little Elk Indian named Henry Jim is obviously an early attempt to develop one of the plots that he ultimately worked into the fabric of his final novel.

In this short story, the agent's name is Glenn Morse, which suggests that it may have been written before McNickle settled upon the name Rafferty. This is not conclusive proof of the story's date of origin; however, the events one finds in it emerge from the same era as his first novel, and they are closely related to those of the other drafts of *Wind* as well as the finished novel. Moreover, the story posits some of the very basic questions concerning Native thought that McNickle explores in *Wind*—and thus is an enlightening point of departure for a study of the novel's concerns.

"Snowfall" tells the story of Henry Jim's death but from the perspective of Morse, whose long years of association with Henry Jim's people have taught him a great deal about Native beliefs and made him question his own. Henry Jim comes to him to request permission to sell his prize horse team to cover his outstanding debts. When Morse offers to loan him the money rather than let him lose such a valuable possession, he learns why the man needs to settle his affairs instead of initiating new ones. Henry Jim has been told in a dream that he is about to die; in fact, he has been told that he will die when the first snow falls the ensuing winter. The parallel with Catharine's dream is obvious, but here—after McNickle had already worked out the details of hers and published them—is an interesting, unequivocal exploration of the connection between dream and reality. When Morse tells his wife about Henry Jim's visit and dream, he adds his own insights into Native consciousness:

> "You see, Clare, they're not like us. The earth is more real to them—much. They're barely separated from it—each generation is born back to it, while we get farther away all the time. Seasons don't mean much to us—we get strawberries in January and freeze ice in July. . . . But these children—I don't like the word—are ever-lastingly sensitive. The least cloud in a summer sky is full of meaning. We call them fatalists, but perhaps their fatalism is hidden knowledge. I wouldn't be sure. Perhaps they understand signs and forbodings which have gone out of our ken. . . ."[4]

The line between the fatalistic vision of the early draft of *The Surrounded* and the self-deterministic one of the published work is clearly drawn here, but one wonders if McNickle is using Morse to mouth what might very well amount to the romantic perception some people possess of these "children." No easy resolution presents itself immediately. However, one cannot help but remember the diary entry in which McNickle revels in the turn of the seasons, the movements of the sun, the world around him. Also, if this story is considered in the context of McNickle's other writings, and in particular the letter to Henon, some interesting associations can be drawn.

Later, Morse visits Henry Jim. As he sits by the obviously ailing man, he begins to wonder:

> Could it be, maybe, that dream and reality were not everlastingly opposed, that they might be but different phases of the one substance? That you could dream yourself into death as readily as you

could will to live? . . . He could not know. But he could guess that
there was in them [Native peoples] an overpowering sense of continuity, of things coming to them whole-made out of the past,
against which their wills and their emotions never warred.[5]

These are the same questions posed to readers of *The Surrounded*,
Runner in the Sun, and *Wind from an Enemy Sky*. Is there a unique
sense of reality for Native peoples? Do they have an inherited
responsiveness to forces that move in their landscapes to which they
have "shaped their lives," a sensitivity that more recent immigrants
and their descendants lack? If one considers McNickle's letter to
Henon in which he ties Native survival directly to their adaptability
and their aspiration "to live in harmony with nature," and if one
considers the dramatic shift in McNickle's own beliefs when he
discarded his fatalistic vision for one which recognized long-standing patterns of self-determination, the message to be found in Mc-
Nickle's fiction is clear. He believed that ancient ways to power and
knowledge may still work to guide contemporary tribal peoples.
"Snowfall" ends with a snow storm, Henry Jim dies, and the prophetic nature of dream is affirmed.

Moreover, McNickle dramatizes the relationship between Native
peoples and their world in the early drafts of the novel itself. One
handwritten manuscript possesses the seeds of the cultural conflict
that provides one of the two main plots of the final work. In this
early draft, however, the story of the Feather Boy bundle is told
solely from the perspective of Rafferty, the Agent who works dili-
gently, and against the orders of his superiors in Washington, to get
the bundle returned. He is successful, but, on the day scheduled for
its return, events take an interesting turn.

A large crowd gathers for the ceremony, and in a scene reminiscent of the Dance in *The Surrounded*, townspeople come to see the
"Indian Show," as they call it. As the Little Elk people and Bull, their
leader, wait, they sing the song of Feather Boy:

"This wind—he-ye, he-ye, he-yo!
This wind blowing—he-ye, he-ye, he-yo!
This wind blowing along my way—he-ye, he-ye, he-yo!
Blowing across the world—he-ye, he-ye, he-yo!
Happily I sing, he-ye, he-ye, he-yo!"[6]

And then the narrator notes how the numerous repetitions of the song begin to blend together to become "just what the song said (for those who understood)—the wind blowing across the world."[7] Immediately, the plane bearing the bundle drops into the narrow valley, as if summoned by the song. The bundle is presented to Bull, and "the last rain god of the Hanging Mountain Clan" returns home.

The descriptive detail of this passage is highly suggestive, but the conclusion to the ceremony goes far beyond suggestion. The bundle is opened. Although, uncharacteristically, Rafferty is given that honor, only Bull looks at the bundle's contents, as is appropriate to his status and the bundle's power, a power made immediately apparent. Bull makes sure of the contents, then sings the Feather Boy song again, and the world responds:

> And then, to the utter consternation of everyone, a strong wind blew up suddenly, coming out of the west. When they looked up, they saw that [great] clouds were piling over the barren sand hills, rolling across the sky. Dust flurries struck forcefully against the startled faces of the spectators.
> The distant thunder sounded, like a great sea pounding beyond the mountains.[8]

Feather Boy is home, to be sure. Thunderbird is coming. If his coming is not obvious, McNickle's description of Bull's response is. He smiles at Rafferty:

> It was a wonderful smile, suggesting that Bull was now in possession of one of the secrets of the universe. It wasn't complacency, but a kind of vindicated pride. Not often in any man's lifetime was it possible to point to one's god and say, Behold![9]

It must be noted that McNickle crossed out the phrase "possession of one of the secrets of the universe" and penned "league with the universe" above it. This minor revision marks the reciprocity inherent in the relationship he envisions and describes. It also emphasizes the fact that at this early stage of the creation of his novel he chose to portray, overtly and without reservation, the power of the knowledge possessed by his Native characters. This portrayal changed, obviously, over the ensuing decades of revision. By the time of the novel's publication, he had significantly muted the "mystical" quality of the relationship between his characters and their world, but he still suggests that it exists for those who search for it.

In *Wind*, McNickle redefines the term "metaphysics" by showing how the physical and the spiritual are connected within Native consciousness. The novel and its early drafts are much more complex than "Snowfall"; the book expands the conflict between two systems of government found in the short story by providing an elaborate history of, and commentary on, the relationship between the federal government and Native peoples. Some critics, such as Louis Owens, argue that this conflict between two cultures is the central theme of the novel and that the tragedy of the conflict derives from the miscommunication between two peoples. Once again, this is an accurate yet limited reading of McNickle's fiction. For Owens and others, *Wind* is a conventional protest novel about the demise of Native cultures. It is not. To see the distinction, one must consider the text's tribal point of view, which is not as fatalistic as some critics would have us believe; protest serves two audiences, and in different ways. For the characters in the novel and for tribal readers alike, the influence of federal strictures is only one aspect of a much more important course of events and complex matrix of problems. For the characters, the power of external, governmental policies is symptomatic of internal or spiritual illness.

As in his first novel, McNickle simultaneously depicts two sequences of events: one that is Native and derives from verbal arts, and one that is Euramerican and derives from written literatures. By juxtaposing two opposing perceptions of event in *Wind*, he draws the line emphatically and clearly. There is no oscillation here, as in *The Surrounded* where the two perceptions were sometimes simultaneously developed within Archilde. In *Wind*, chapter breaks often mark a shift from one story line to the other—from the story of Bull and his people to that of the Anglo characters. Given the duration of the revision process, this is understandable; McNickle obviously pasted portions of several drafts together, and such clearly defined shifts make the process easier. But it also provides a separate and distinct plot that highlights the physical actions of Native characters and, through isolation, the spiritual bases that motivate them. By the end of the book, actions and their spiritual implications are so intricately entwined that they cannot be separated. Again, as in his other novels, this continuity is provided by the actions of one pivotal character.

Although Antoine lacks the schizophrenia of Archilde's dual educations, he, too, has been away to the government boarding school. He has not returned unscathed, but any threats to Antoine's identity—any attraction to move in ways unlike his people—have been put to rest by his active particpation in a ceremonial dance. Like Mike in the earlier novel, he has shared in his people's movements and been cured of the fear that haunts his dreams. Nevertheless, as with Archilde and Salt, his ongoing tribal education is the central story in *Wind*, and it is described as a journey. In fact, an interesting aspect of the novel is that, to explicate his education and therefore the book itself, the reader must become concerned with journey and education as process, more than with the product they might achieve.

Although McNickle still intended to educate his reader, his audience had changed over the decades. Forced assimilation was not the heated controversy it was in the 1930s, but the issue of Indian sovereignty was as crucial as ever. Also, the reader of the 1970s had resources unavailable to the reader of 1936. Since that time an increasing number of powerful, and popular, Indian writers had emerged to express their cultures' ways of perceiving events and deciding upon appropriate action.

McNickle's late correspondence contains repeated references to several writers and the works that mark the emergence of modern, written fiction by Native peoples. In one letter he provides a list of books, including N. Scott Momaday's Pulitzer Prize-winning *House Made of Dawn*, for a librarian who wanted to expand her collection.[10] Five years later, in a letter to Elaine Edleman, he cites such recent works as *The Man to Send Rain Clouds* as a valuable "source for young Indian writers."[11] He was well aware of the continuing education of the American public about things Indian and therefore realized that the generalized cultural views and beliefs presented in *Wind* did not need to be slowly and cautiously developed as they were in his first novel. His purpose is the same, however. Like the earlier works, his last demonstrates the processes by which important problems, including threats to tribal survival, may be addressed. Problems change; the process of resolution persists.

Like the Salish, the Little Elk people are surrounded and they must watch the erosion of their traditional power. But, as in the earlier novel, blame is not to be placed solely on the world "outside." A great deal of the loss to the Salish and Little Elk Indians can be attributed to European conquest and colonization; they fought for their land and lost. But the Salish contributed to their dilemma by sending for the priests, at their own peril. As the story of *Wind* unfolds, it becomes clear that the Little Elk ability to deal with such a sweeping change in fortune has also been hampered by misunderstanding and therefore inappropriate behavior within the tribe.

The main event of the story transpires thirty years prior to the events described in the novel, when Enemy Horse—the Little Elk leader—defied tradition and named his second son, Bull, as his successor rather than his eldest son. The eldest son moved from their mountain stronghold to the valley floor, where he received his allotment of land from the federal government and adopted the lifeway dictated by the Indian Agency. He changed his name to Henry Jim and, in an act of defiance, gave his people's most sacred medicine bundle—the Feather Boy bundle—to a Protestant missionary, who in turn sent it to a museum in the East. Although Bull remains in the mountains with those of his band who did not follow Henry Jim and continues to live a traditional lifeway, he is the leader of a people sorely divided and at the mercy of forces in the world beyond their control. The brothers' enmity is at the heart of the people's problems, and the events of the novel describe their reconciliation.

Interestingly, Henry Jim's behavior derives from what McNickle considered the major flaws in the allotment system, under which reservation lands were sectioned and distributed to tribal members. After all, he had firsthand knowledge of the system and its effects on people. He sold his own allotment in 1925 in order to study at Oxford, and the early draft of *Wind* includes a lengthy condemnation of the system, which suggests one way he rationalized his choice to sell his "own" acreage. The system was designed "to make individuals of the Indians."[12] Allotments jeopardized Native cultures' sense of community and therefore their ability to survive. Fragmenting a land results in the fragmentation of a people. Henry Jim's actions are those of an individual, and the results of actions based upon a misled sense of individuality are disastrous. In physical terms, tribal lands were often sold to whites and therefore lost to the people; their spirituality suffered accordingly, as old beliefs and ways were sacrificed by people trying to conform to a new culture. There are ways to reintegrate, though, as McNickle demonstrates.

In the very first sentence of *Wind*, he gives the central structuring device for his narrative: "The Indian named Bull and his grandson took a walk into the mountains to look at a dam built in a cleft of rock, and what began as a walk became a journey into the world."[13] Bull and his band have lived in virtual isolation in the mountains, but the forces at work in the world finally threaten even this secluded land. A modern hydroelectric project has "killed" their river, as Bull puts it, and channeled its water into an irrigation system built for the benefit of the Anglo farmers who have purchased reservation land. Bull's thirty years of removal from the affairs of his people—his whole people—and his refusal to address changes in their world have contributed to their continued loss of control over their tribal lands, and therefore their future. The old ways of directing their lives and therefore of control have been subverted by anger—the epitome of a lack of control—and the initial point at which Bull's and Antoine's short walk becomes a journey is clearly, violently defined.

As the two approach the heights above the dam, Antoine remembers a lesson he learned about this specific spot where his people formerly held their summer dance. "It had been a holy place, this mountain-locked meadow. 'Be careful what you do here,' the boy had been told by his relatives. 'This is a place of power. Be careful what you think. Keep your thoughts good' " (5). The boy's perception, as he walks through his people's landscape, is enlightened by their stories and ceremonial beliefs, and he heeds the warnings associated with this one, particular place. But Bull does not. As his grandfather views the dam, Antoine senses that a significant event is about to occur: "The shadows were deep in Bull's face, and burning lights seemed to dance in his eyes. The boy watched, knowing that something would happen" (6). Bull loses control and, out of anger, fires his rifle twice into the dam, and then shouts his frustration. Who has killed the river? "Is he two-legged like other men? Or is he a monster first-man, who decides things in his own way?" (7)

Any reader with knowledge of American history can, of course, answer. The builder is one who "decides things in his own way." As McNickle notes in his correspondence with his publisher, "*One* of the central themes of the novel is the story of government-Indian relations, and in particular, the high-handed, but legal, manner in which Indians were robbed of their land and water" (emphasis added).[14] But this is only one of the stories in the novel and, as in *The Surrounded*, it is ancillary to the larger story of the Indians' reaction to the changes taking place in their world. How is one to respond to this legalized thievery of one's sacred things, the land and the water? Bull's immediate response is anger, as were many others' in early encounters with the Euramerican. However, the inappropriateness of such actions is immediately apparent as he turns: "He stopped then. He had seen his grandson and saw his eyes bright with fear. And his eyes no longer bulged" (7). One of the effects of conquest is that "the white man makes us forget our holy places. He makes us small" (9). To be large again—to have the power to move the world—one must employ the beliefs that have traditionally provided control and power. The sacred places must be remembered and visited with respect; the rituals and ceremonies that exercise power must be practiced with reverence for correct, perfect action; the stories must be articulated for the young; and people must live by the value systems evolved over epochs of history. McNickle conveys this pantribal message through the events of the novel.

A ceremony, the Dance, is one of the central, and most revealing, events in *The Surrounded*. McNickle's clearest insight about Salish lifeways centers on the ways they move in the dance, but also personally, daily. As Catharine prepares Narcisse for the Dance, Archilde realizes that the motions of her hands say a great deal about her inner state and that "in a matter so simple, the least part has its significance or it is all meaningless."[15] Similarly, in *Runner in the Sun* McNickle shows how the actions of one individual on a quest become the actions of all his people through the story that will be told of his journey in their oral literature and through the ceremony that is the result.

McNickle's vision about these types of enlightened movement is the very heart of *Wind from an Enemy Sky*. Journey is motion, and the events of the novel—the happenings that mark significant aspects of Bull's and Antoine's movements—show that journey may be simultaneously physical and mythical, that the two realms are inseparable, and that this perception is an integral aspect of the way the Little Elk Indians view their world. Journey, after all, is a series of necessary decisions about how to move next, and decisions are based upon a body of knowledge and custom. This heightened narrative emphasis on motion is provided by the observations of an "outsider," the perceptive Indian Agent Rafferty, but insights into the implications of such a view of motion are given by the numerous rides of the major Indian characters which depict or imply a standard that is craftily restated with each phase of the journey of Bull and Antoine.

Agent Rafferty is an interesting character. In many ways he and Adam Pell—the multimillionaire engineer who financed and designed the dam (and who is patterned after George Heye)—are separate aspects of the character of Father Grepilloux in McNickle's first novel. Rafferty is a social worker turned bureaucrat, and he demonstrates a perceptive sympathy for the Little Elk people. Rather than impose his notions of how the world—and the Agency—should work, however, he is content to observe patiently the Indians' actions and thereby learn how best to act in support of their needs. In this way he reflects McNickle's own actions over the years as he worked as a liaison between Native peoples and civic and governmental agencies, and he is the antithesis of Pell, who professes a sympathy and understanding for the Indians but continually acts—with what he considers their best interests at heart—to their harm. As Bull correctly guesses, Pell is one who is used to deciding things in his own way, but the construction of the dam is only one example of his cultural myopia. Rafferty's observations, like those of Morse in "Snowfall," give the broad cultural audience for whom McNickle writes a framework and point of reference by which to understand the actions of the Little Elk people. This framework is fleshed out with the Indian lifeways McNickle presents in the events he describes.

At almost exactly the physical center of the book, McNickle describes a trip taken by Rafferty and Doc Edwards (the Agency doctor) to visit Henry Jim's farm. Henry Jim has summoned them to explain his people's need for the return of the medicine bundle and to enlist the agent's aid. In order to explain the importance of the search, however, Henry Jim must tell a story, his story, and as it is told Rafferty watches the actions of The Boy—his Indian driver and interpreter—and learns something of significance about the Little Elk people:

> Rafferty watched The Boy's deft movements as he worked on the fire—the delicate touch of the large hands, the ease of the crouch—and he could see the fitness of the man in his situation. What a man learned, and it was all he learned in a lifetime, was a degree of fitness for the things he had to do. . . . Here in a tepee world, the parts fitted together. The people had grace and understanding; their acts were competent. (125)

His insight echoes that of Archilde as he watches his mother prepare for the Dance, and the concept of motion that McNickle presents is such an integral part of the lifeways he describes that often only outsiders may note it and comment upon it, even if they cannot fully comprehend its significance.

McNickle was an outsider both because he left his family and land to travel in the world and because he was a storyteller and visionary, one of those who traditionally move beyond their immediate societies in order to clarify beliefs and to provide objectivity and knowledge. As outsiders, Archilde and Rafferty are also fit commentators. Later in *Wind*, Rafferty's flash of recognition has developed into a clearer awareness of a central aspect of the people's way of life:

> Quite suddenly, and effortlessly it now seemed, he [Rafferty] had begun to get the feel of their perspective of the world. It had something to do with motion, with the way they gestured, their facial movements, and the way they walked—he had glimpsed it for the first time the day he watched The Boy mending the fire, and only partially absorbed it. Later it grew large in his mind. But there seemed to be a still larger aspect, and this he did not yet under-

stand. It had to do with their way of talking, and that followed
habits bred in the senses themselves and made the world the way it
is to a seeing and hearing and feeling man. (176)

He comes very close to understanding the people he has been
assigned to guide. What he cannot comprehend is the way that
motion and language work together with other aspects of the Little
Elk Indians' existence to become their lifeway, a connection he
might have made had he listened to Henry Jim's stories and tried to
understand them in relationship to the people and their ways of
reacting to circumstances. The reader, however, is given the connections necessary for this comprehension through McNickle's presentation of the events that mark the journey of Bull and his grandson.

The importance of learning the correct ways to move is stated
early in *Wind*. Throughout the description of the climb to the dam,
McNickle emphasizes the quality of Antoine's movements as his
grandfather tries to teach him how to move appropriately in the
world. As the two walk, the boy's movements are still "uncertain"
and "coltish" as he, literally, follows in his grandfather's moccasin
prints. He lacks control, but he recognizes that one may learn it in a
number of ways:

> But even without words, to travel with a man like his grandfather
> was to learn much. You watched how his moccasins met the
> ground and you found it very tiring. The foot never struck the loose
> pebbles, always avoided the dry twig. You followed the example,
> but you lost your balance, crashed into a bush, scattered stones. (4)

One way to learn is by example from one who knows, just as the
Salish learn from Sinchlep/Coyote how to make clothes, kill game
for food, and use medicinal plants. But Bull's actions at the dam are
hardly "balanced" either, and they both recognize the impropriety
of the act.

On their trip homeward, Bull stops to rest and to offer some
words of advice that are repeated throughout the novel and enlighten its conclusion: "Grandson, when a man goes someplace,
whether to hunt or to visit relatives, he should think about the
things he sees, or maybe the words someone speaks to him. He asks
himself, What did I learn from this? What should I remember?" (8)

This description of a traditional responsibility provides the boy with the proper perception for viewing the major events of the novel, including the final confrontation. The same perception was given to Salt by the Holy One in *Runner in the Sun* and aided him in his quest. Antoine will see much and remember it all, in particular the events that result from their walk to the dam and the enmity of two brothers, which has complicated the people's lives and threatened their survival.

Henry Jim takes the initial step toward reconciliation, a move traditionally the duty of the younger brother. He is aware of the dangers coming from the world outside, and he knows what must be done. The people must once again become united and the old ways reaffirmed by the return of the medicine bundle and its ceremonies. Like so many of McNickle's characters, Henry Jim has had a dream that provides him with the knowledge of what is to come. As a result of that dream he quickly and easily renounces the way of life he has lived for decades and turns once again to the old beliefs, just as Catharine did in *The Surrounded*. The humility of his gesture at reconciliation has its effect. Bull and the other men accept his counsel as if no time had elapsed since he left, and the people become one again. The second step in the journey of Antoine, its second event, has taken place; he has met his uncle who, like him, possesses a power. The resolution to a course of action is achieved through communal reason and discussion and one man's efforts. This event is of obvious significance in the stories of Bull and Henry Jim, but also of major importance in the story of the Little Elk people.

With Henry Jim's ride homeward after the meeting, McNickle gives his first, succinct demonstration of the mode in which movement may become one with language (articulation) but also with memory, mythology, philosophy, and, it is implied, even more. This type of responsible movement is necessary if the people are to survive. As he rides, his eyes closed "keeping a vision within," he sings a song:

> The song was old, telling of a time when a boy listened eagerly
> for voices, wherever they might be, the voices of men, of the wind,
> of stars moving through the night.

A time when a boy came to a campfire and when men were talking in the shadows, their voices rising to laughter, falling away before a drumbeat, coming strong again.

A time when the dawn lay in dampness on the prairie grass, and cooking fires were starting up, the smoke a blessing power.

A time when a grandfather explained the tracks along the trail, pointed out where the eagle nested, and showed how to cleanse the body in the sweat bath.

A time when the plover cried and the song of the meadowlark wove the world together.

And bitter times! When the belly hungered and quaked. When winter sickness came and people tumbled dazed out of their tepees. When quarrels rose to sharp, hard tones and children ran to their mothers' skirts. A gun spoke in firs and there was blood on a gooseberry bush. And the soldiers dragged guns over the road and turned them toward the people.

The song was without end in the mind of the old man on the horse. (29)

As he moves through his world, his dutiful song engages his memory and it redefines his relationship and responsibilities to that world. In this brief passage, McNickle establishes the primal ways to the knowledge of how to act in light of the current problem facing Henry Jim's people: through a personal relationship with a spirit or *somesh* in the "natural" world (a voice from the wind or stars); or through communal action around the campfires of people who are unified in a way of life, as in the meeting Henry Jim has just left; or through example, much as Antoine learns from Bull.

But even in this seemingly placid moment, conflict and potential loss are present. At the heart of the song there is strife: bitter words, death, and the people's subjugation by the U.S. Army. This bleak history is as integral a part of his memory—the things that have been seen, heard, and remembered by a people—as the idyllic images that precede it, and the final sentence is a statement of the Salish perception of the world found in their oral literature and McNickle's first novel. The world is mutable, and sometimes changes come that are not beneficial. But the people survive if they remember the power to be derived from their obligations. The fact that the song is sung by the person who had originally adapted to the new ways of the European immigrants is significant; even for him the old ways persist to guide and instruct. Guns speak and individuals fall, but the people go on (a lesson important to the reader at the end of the book). The song is without end, because the life journey of the people has not ended; their song continues because Henry Jim perpetuates it through his act of articulation. As long as the song is sung, the people will live, and this assertion is reenforced by McNickle's use of two other songs.

Henry Jim's trip to Bull's camp was initiated and made urgent by his own personal vision, given him in a dream. He has heard "the grass speaking" to him and knows that his days are numbered. Despite his thirty years as the Agency's model citizen, this character's ability to derive knowledge through a personal relationship with some obscure force in the world around him—his *somesh* or medicine—still exists; his guardian is still an active participant in and guide to his life. After his visit with his brother, Henry Jim rides to the camps of his kin in the valley to tell them of the reconciliation and the resolution to ask Rafferty to act in their behalf to regain the Feather Boy bundle. And as he sleeps in the lodge of one kinsman, Iron Child, he dreams again. In this dream, the grass sings to him once more and he hears the songs of the plover and the meadowlark; then a voice speaks to him: "Now you must sing the song you heard long ago. Don't stop. Keep singing. Otherwise I will not be able to help you. When you stop singing, you will float away and be one of us" (55). His guide intervenes in his behalf and tells him exactly what he needs to do to live. Henry Jim's personal power song must be sung to keep him alive, and again articulation is tied to physical effect: survival. From this moment on in the narrative, either he or his kin sings it. He dies only after he has fulfilled his part in the search for the bundle, has seen his people unified once again, and has learned that Bull will accept the aid of Rafferty.

The story of Henry Jim's prophetic dream of death remains from "Snowfall" and from the manuscript, but here, it lacks the emphatic, overt explanation provided in either the short story or the "Indian Agent." Its point is nonetheless the same: there are sources of knowledge and ways to knowledge that have evolved from the close alignment of the movements and actions of humankind on this continent with the environments they have inhabited for thousands of years, and this alignment is given careful statement in the novel.

Throughout, the Little Elk people seem to be in perpetual motion—riding to the Agency, to Henry Jim's or Bull's camp—and this continual activity and the manner in which it is accomplished further emphasize McNickle's concept of responsive action. As the leaders ride to the Agency, they sing Henry Jim's song. Like a ceremony, this act is a communal responsibility, and it unites the people by concentrating their efforts on a shared activity that derives from, and reinforces, a shared pattern of belief. In the Salish story of "The Ram's Horn Tree," a song's articulation is the means by which Sinchlep/Coyote taps a power in the world by concentrating his mental and physical movements on the basis and nature of that power. The same idea is presented within the context of the novel—and it works. Henry Jim lives through the power of his song, but communal responsibilities go beyond group activities. When he is alone, his identification with his people is reaffirmed in the way he reacts to the things he sees, hears, and remembers. This communal duty is stated at the outset by Bull; it is demonstrated by Henry Jim's ride and song as he returns from Bull's camp; and it is depicted once again when Antoine rides to the Indian Agency to join Bull and his men.

As Antoine rides, one sees McNickle's belief of what constitutes, as Rafferty phrases it, "a seeing and hearing and feeling man," and it is a scene that has strong overtones of McNickle's diary entries that record his own sensitivity to the simple, natural movements of the world around him, even when he lived in New York City:

> It was a time of pleasure, to be riding in the early morning air, to feel the drumming earth come upward through the pony's legs and enter his own flesh. Yes, the earth power coming into him as he moved over it. And a thing of the air, like a bird. He breathed deeply of the bird-air, and that was power too. He held his head high, a being in flight. And he sang, as his people sang, of the gray rising sun and the shadows that were only emerging from the night.
>
> To be one among his people, to grow up in their respect, to be his grandfather's kinsman—this was power in itself, the power that flows between people and makes them one. He could feel it now, a

healing warmth that flowed into his center from many-reaching
body parts.
    Still, he had no shell of hardness around him. (106)

As he moves through the landscape, Antoine marks the potential
sources of sustenance, of potential healing power, that he perceives
in his world. There is earth power, the power of the bird-air, and the
power of belonging to his people. But a person must do more than
just learn to recognize the powers at work in the world; he or she
must articulate this recognition and respect. Antoine sings, and as a
result his travels go beyond a physical movement from one point to
another in the land. Like Henry Jim's ride earlier, Antoine's becomes
the celebration of a lifeway: a relationship between a people and a
landscape and a pattern of belief that enlightens the people's knowledge of how, and when, to act. This pantribal representation is far
removed from the dull, naked, fatalistic savage of "The Hungry
Generations." McNickle's vision is sharp and clear at such moments.
    Yet, as one sees in Henry Jim's song, memories do not contain
only pleasant things. As Antoine sings, his experiences at Chemawa
arise to darken his ride. In particular, he remembers the Marching
Captain: the Bureau of Indian Affairs' Indian drill instructor. To a
boy such as Antoine who, as McNickle carefully notes, was raised in
a tradition in which children are rarely punished and in which there
is no word for "disciplinarian," the Marching Captain symbolizes all
the meanness that can inhabit the world. And yet, when the Marching Captain cries at the news of the death of Antoine's mother,
Antoine suddenly realizes that the Marching Captain is an Indian,
like himself, and that behind this symbol of his fears lives a person
who has become "small," who has gained a position of authority
through individual initiative but suppressed his identity. He is no
real threat; nothing lasting is built on fear. What begins as a dark
memory becomes an affirmation. Antoine has lived in the Anglo
world; he learned from what he has seen, heard, and remembered.
He can survive, and the fear he briefly feels because of his ride
toward another authoritarian figure of the white world—the Indian
Agency—dissolves. The song comes to him again, even more
strongly: "By the time he came in sight of the government's white
buildings, his head was high" (110). There are many threats to a

person, and a people, in the world; what McNickle considers important is the ways one deals with them.

Antoine lacks the "shell of hardness" which is characteristic of his
grandfather. He is open to the forces and sources in the world
around him; Bull has closed himself within his angry and inflexible
resolution. The old man's actions over the years have not been those
expected of a leader of a people faced with great peril, yet resources
are available to him—just as they are to Henry Jim—to regain the
control his people have lost over the years, control they require to
survive. Once again, McNickle uses a ride to the agency to show
how Bull's relationship with the land differs from that of his brother
and grandson.

As they ride, Bull's thoughts tell his dilemma:

> Journeys can be long and difficult, and Bull was finding it so, al-
> though they had only five miles to travel to reach Little Elk Agency.
> But he was traveling through time and over mountains and prairies
> of thought and feeling. Until his brother had come to his camp on a
> certain night, he had lived in a waiting world. . . .
> A journey could be difficult beyond endurance, when a man had
> to travel with himself and bring into his thoughts the bad actions of
> a lifetime. (129)

Interestingly, his thoughts travel—through space and time—and
thus perform a similar role to Modeste's story at Catharine's feast in
The Surrounded. Through his reminiscences one sees the story of the
Little Elk people's loss of power, and at the center of his memory and
their loss lies the anger and "bad actions" that have isolated Bull
from his people.

As he looks at his grandson who rides beside him, he wonders
how he might spare the boy the angry thoughts that have consumed
him. Although aware, he still harbors such thoughts. He feels that
his people should have made a final, prideful stand against the
Europeans: "If we had only killed a few, they would have come with
their big guns and killed us all. They would be walking over our
heads today, but we wouldn't have to care anymore" (136). His
anger and sense of loss lead him to view communal suicide as
preferable to survival, at least survival in the static terms he perceives. He lives in the past, unable to cope with change, and this

propensity—as McNickle presents it—is self-centered, stupid, and disastrous. His message for contemporary Native peoples is obvious. As Bull rides to the Agency, he does not sing a song to celebrate the present, and the ride ends not with an affirmation but with violent thoughts. His journey, begun and perpetuated in anger, continues toward its logical conclusion.

Henry Jim, however, has another vision, and it is based upon deliberate action to ensure survival. His move to reunite his people on a quest for the bundle is "a thing he had to do—afterwards, a different time would come. *A different time would come . . .*" (53). The world is dynamic, and the people may initiate transformations. What remains to be seen is the nature of the change that Henry Jim knows must come. Properly attended to, it may be beneficial; guided by anger and a sense of irretrievable loss, it will be harmful. The "big guns" may still be used against them. It is a tenuous existence, Henry Jim shows us; therefore, it is imperative that great care and restraint be taken in the actions, thoughts, and speech used in the search for the bundle. Unfortunately, as McNickle shows, sufficient control over individual actions is difficult in today's world, in which stupidity and therefore frustration abound.

What would seem at first a simple task—find the bundle and ask for its return—becomes immediately complicated as Bull and Antoine's journey progresses. After Henry Jim's visit, Bull leaves camp to travel the land, like his brother, to bring word of the reconciliation. While he is gone, his nephew, Pock Face, makes his own journey to the dam, with Bull's rifle, a trip that carefully parallels Bull's. As he stands on the spot where Bull vented his anger the day before, he sees a man climb a scaffolding. Like Bull, Pock Face acts impulsively in a sacred place. He kneels, takes aim, and fires; the man falls dead. As Pock Face returns to camp, snow falls to cover the deed. He is content in his belief that he has killed the man who killed the river and thereby avenged his people's loss.

He is very nearly correct, for he has killed Adam Pell's nephew. His nephew's death brings Pell to the reservation, where he learns of the Little Elk Indians' reactions to the dam and of their search for the Feather Boy bundle. Like Rafferty, he becomes an active force in their search, for the bundle was sent to a New York museum funded, in large part, by him. The story of the dam and the story of the bundle, which are already inseparably intertwined in the minds of the Little Elk people, merge for the Anglo characters as well. Both become the means by which McNickle demonstrates "the high-handed, but legal" ways the Indians have been robbed of tribal lands and water rights, but also the ways that they may control their own lives and their futures. Moreover, the investigation into the murder provides focal points where the Indians' perception of events contrasts with those of the Anglo characters.

For McNickle's audience in the 1970s, Adam Pell becomes an interesting character. Along with the increased Euramerican awareness of Native cultures and issues had come an increase in the numbers of people who wanted "to help," help quite often translating into reactions similar to Father Grepilloux's in *The Surrounded*. After Pell returns to New York following the inquest into his nephew's death, he begins to research the history of the dam he built in the belief he was helping the Little Elk people. He finds the systematic plundering of their land under the auspices of materially improving their lifestyle. Through fifty years of Congressional manipulation under the direction of numerous administrations, the power brokers of Washington have siphoned off the wealth from reservation land, including its water. Obviously, McNickle provides his readers with nothing new, historically. Instead, the facts provide the emotionally charged sense of wrong designed to attract his readers deeper into his primary lesson: an understanding of how, and why, the Indians react as they do.

It is the history of governmental dealings with the Indians that McNickle wishes to expose with this subplot. In a letter to Alain Henon, mentioned earlier, he expresses his understanding of the ethnocentric perceptions that allowed such blatant exploitation to occur. After he notes the adaptability of Native peoples, he concludes that their faith in the cycles of nature made them more optimistic about the future than their European counterparts: "The Europeans called this improvident and they labored to correct the trait. But what they conceived of as a character fault was, in Indian terms, the way of reason."[16] The attempts by Euramericans to correct the supposed fault led to loss for Native peoples, as the immigrants showed the Native how to make the land perform as they thought it should. Such a sense of dominance runs counter to the Native perception of the relationship between humankind and the land, as symbolized in the book by the medicine bundle. Unfortunately, the bundle has not survived thirty years of storage in a mouse-infested basement.[17]

The central story of the bundle coincides with the story of individuals throughout Bull and Antoine's journey. Unfortunately for the Little Elk people, their true leader, Henry Jim, dies before the search is completed, and the full weight of the responsibility falls to Bull. And Bull is an angry man. For years, the old medicine man Two Sleeps has gone into the mountains to listen to the voices of storms to learn how the people may regain control of their own destiny. He returns with the information necessary for Bull to act responsibly and to reunite his people, but Bull accuses Two Sleeps of meddling, and "in anger he went himself to the mountains and had no vision of his own" (130). His anger has severed him from traditional ways to knowledge. He refuses to accept counsel from one who knows the correct steps to take, and his anger also limits his ability to derive knowledge from his own relationship with the powers, the voices, found in the natural world. He is almost completely without resources, and even the stories that have traditionally provided yet another way to knowledge no longer aid him.

During the winter following the reconciliation and Henry Jim's death, McNickle gives further evidence of the ways by which a people may maintain control, or lose it, through angry and hasty acts. In many Native traditions, winter is the time for storytelling; since travel is nearly impossible, Bull's people are content to stay near their fires and travel with their minds. This winter, the stories told all focus on one overriding question: what is to happen to the Little Elk people? Obviously, the same question has been asked by all Native peoples since the incursion of the European. Significantly, McNickle ties the question to the telling of the Feather Boy bundle story, which is told for Antoine who has journeyed out into the world and culture that surround his people. His return from school has brought life back to the camp: "A people needed young ones who would put the sun back in the sky" (204). As Modeste demonstrates in *The Surrounded*, the future lies in the ability of the grandchildren to adapt, to respond, but still move as a community; they must be told the stories that unite the people, define their beliefs and lead, therefore, to survival. As Bull tells the story, however, the reader begins to note a similarity between the events it relates and those of Bull's own story.

He tells Antoine that Sun has a child named Thunderbird, who once saw the people starving, took pity on them, and, disregarding his father's warnings not to interfere, came to the people as a baby born to a young girl of the tribe. His rapid growth marked him as exceptional, and the people were suspicious of him, much as the Salish feared Spokani when he came to them in the story of the Sun. No one would speak to him, "which wasn't the way Thunderbird planned it, and it almost spoiled everything" (206). He asked his mother again and again what it was the people needed most. She— who had felt the smart of ignorance and the derision of her people— would not answer impulsively but chose to think upon the question instead. Her mother, however, believing the answer to be obvious, told him that the people needed food more than anything else. To fulfill this need, Thunderbird undertook a journey to the south and collected seeds from various food plants, as well as tobacco. On his flight homeward, however, he began to reconsider the peoples' actions and decided that "they think too much about eating, and they are mean" (207). What they needed most, as his mother well knew, was good hearts. So Thunderbird dropped the seeds along his route, returning only with tobacco.

The people became angry, but he scolded them for their ingratitude. He has brought them "the most powerful present of all" and it will aid them in becoming a dynamic force in their world:

> It [tobacco smoke] will rise upward like your breath, like a prayer. If you have this smoke, you won't need those other plants. In time, they will all come to you. The buffalo and all game animals will come to you. If you need rain to make your crops grow, just let this smoke rise from your pipe and it will come to you. (208)

Through the faithful practice of the pipe ceremony he brought them, the people received the things they needed; they were in control. These things *came to them* when the correct ceremonial actions were taken. As Thunderbird left, he bestowed his bundle on "his mother, who had never been angry with him" (208). The story's message about anger and hasty judgment is clear, and, as Bull finishes telling it, he once again looks to Antoine and "saw his grandson's eyes shining with wonder" (208).

Unlike his grandfather, the boy is learning a great deal on his journey, and the night of storytelling is the third event along his way as he begins to understand his world. McNickle is careful throughout the narrative to emphasize Antoine's sensitivity to what he sees, hears, and experiences. As noted on his ride to the Agency, Antoine feels the powers of the world move within him. Also, when Henry Jim visits Bull's camp, the boy offers him his hand, and, when they touch, Antoine feels "an unexpected flow of warmth and strength pull at him" (16). When he visits Henry Jim's camp later, the scene is reconstructed with the old man offering his hand in turn. Antoine feels "the knotted bones and the sinuous clasp, the dry warmth, and as on that other night he was filled with wonder" (116). He recognizes almost intuitively the personal power of his kinsman, his uncle, and Antoine's power is recognized, as well, by Henry Jim, the man with a vision of the future: "You will be a strong man. . . . It is here in your hand. Even now your strength passes to me, as it will pass to your people when the time comes" (116). And the time is near.

Like his predecessors Archilde and Salt, Antoine is a "seeing and hearing and feeling man" who has been to the outside world and returned without the shell of hardness that limits his grandfather. He is the hope of his people, one who, like a hero of old, may indeed perform feats as impossible as putting the sun back into the sky for them. He participates in ceremonies and the major events of the novel, hears the stories of his people, sees examples of appropriate and inappropriate actions, and remembers it all. From his journey, he gains the strength to survive the final confrontation in the novel and to provide an alternative to Bull's limited, suicidal perception or the equally dangerous assimilation.

The final scene in the novel dramatically brings the two plots together. As Owens notes, the event hinges upon misunderstanding through miscommunication. The Indians' reactions are as Rafferty feared, and wholly justified for McNickle's readers. Shocked and then angered at the loss of Feather Boy, Bull takes Louis's rifle and acts on behalf of his people. He kills Pell. When Rafferty steps forward, Bull kills him as well; the seemingly sympathetic ministrations of a bureaucrat do not always result in exoneration. The tribal police officer, The Boy, fulfills his duty also; asking Bull's forgiveness, he kills the old man with a shot to the heart. But is this the death knell for a culture? A fatalistic conflict doomed to be repeated again and again until all Natives are dead or assimilated?

Hardly. It is the death of one Indian whose journey, begun with angry words in a sacred place of power, reaches its logical conclusion in anger and violence. Indeed, the final lines of the novel provide as bleak a statement as those at the end of *The Surrounded*: *"That day, the cry of the plover was heard everywhere. . . . Ke-ree, ke-ree, ke-ree. No meadowlarks sang, and the world fell apart"* (256). But as in McNickle's first novel, the bleakness is not unqualified.

"The world has fallen apart." Interestingly enough, these lines appear in none of the earlier drafts but only set in type in the final galley proof. No correspondence survives in McNickle's papers that directly relates to them. Because the book was published after McNickle's death, one might question whether they were McNickle's or the publisher's addition, but Harper and Row assure "that the corrections made on the manuscript were only the most minor grammatical changes."[18] It might be that McNickle himself inserted the final lines at a very late date by way of a final revision, almost an afterthought, and that no record remains of the addition. Given the main structural device of the book—the progression of Antoine's journey and education—the lines then become an appropriate punctuation for the novel, as well as for McNickle's lifelong effort to educate the American public about things Indian.

To respond to the final scene, readers need to recognize the innate strengths and durability of Native cultures and realize that, perhaps, their unique, long-standing relationship with the landscapes of this continent possesses a logic of endurance that we would all be well advised to understand. In *Wind*, this logic and its inherent faith in the cycles of nature are exemplified by the birds and by Antoine. The meadow lark (traditionally a messenger) and the plover are the two birds consistently referred to, and their songs hold the world together. And the birds survive, as do their songs. The songs sung earlier by Henry Jim and Antoine remain as well.

Although Henry Jim dies, his successor survives. Antoine witnesses the final scene but, like Archilde at the end of *The Surrounded*, takes no physical action. Instead, he participates through an act of understanding. He recognizes the events leading to this point in their journey and understands the motivations of his grandfather. He is still learning from the old man as he watches Bull take the gun. He sees the vision he had when Bull lost his temper at the dam become a reality:

> Antoine saw his grandfather's face in the same instant, and recognized the look of wild dispair. He knew that the thing he had imagined would finally happen. Black blood would spill on the ground. His grandfather would feel strong again, *and the boy was proud of him*. [emphasis added] (255)

By not relying on traditional ways of acting and reacting, Bull dooms himself, but he also provides a valuable lesson—for Anglo and Indian alike. Antoine recognizes his grandfather's need to feel strong again, to feel big, even though he also realizes that Bull's anger will lead inevitably to death.

Despite the hasty actions of individuals, however, the people survive. Quarrels lead to fear and anger that cause guns to speak, but the people endure as they always have, through men of vision like Antoine, Henry Jim, and Two Sleeps. These are the men who pick up the pieces of shattered worlds, grieve for their dead, and tell the stories of Bull and Thunderer and Feather Boy, which will once again mold the pieces into a whole. Only by performing the ceremonies and by telling the stories of past happenings can the people shed light on correct action, and therefore on the resolutions to contemporary problems. In Native verbal arts, life is painted as the fluctuation between chaos and order, between bad times and good, but always both, and McNickle's fiction follows that tradition. Both imply the continuation of Native cultures despite trying times. At the end of *Wind*, the values of Little Elk society—and those of Native cultures in general—prevail despite the final confrontation. Like life itself in times of travail when the future seems bleak and foreboding, the image of dissolution is, paradoxically, qualified and redeemed through the telling. Narrative implies, and nurtures, transcendence.

5 The Vision Today

An analysis of McNickle's contributions to contemporary American Indian written art is problematic, to say the least. His major work, *The Surrounded*, was published, out of print, and forgotten long before most of today's writers were born, let alone at work on their writing careers. McNickle himself could not find copies of it. If his work had a direct influence, it was not widespread until recent times. (In 1983, for instance, Simon Ortiz entitled a collection of short fiction from tribal writers *Earth Power Coming*, a phrase borrowed from the description of Antoine's ride to the Agency in *Wind from an Enemy Sky*.) This is not to suggest, however, that his fiction and that of more recent writers do not share some interesting and revealing qualities. Perhaps this sharing is understandable. He faced the same problems of publication and audience as the generation who followed, and he found similar ways of addressing them.

After McNickle's death, Alfonso Ortiz (1979, 632) wrote a tribute to the writer for the *American Anthropologist*. In it, he provides some appropriate insights into McNickle's narrative power: "D'Arcy used words sparingly and with respect, like traditional Indian orators, and one had to become fully engaged to grasp the subtlety of his perception." Critics would be quick to agree with this statement, if it were applied to any other contemporary Indian writer, but as the early failure of *The Surrounded* and the interpretations of some recent scholars attest, that subtlety is not always recognized in McNickle's work; therefore, his achievements are seldom appreciated. However, even a brief, selective survey of recent Native novels and novelists will demonstrate how truly anticipatory McNickle's voice, derived from his revisions of *The Surrounded*, was.[1]

First, there are some obvious, general parallels. For the most part, recent Native novels begin *in medias res*; many have protagonists who, like Archilde, are of mixed descent; they often rely heavily on Native materials from the writers' own tribal experiences, traditions, and verbal arts to animate and direct their narratives; and many share McNickle's use of the journey, either physical or imaginative/ educational, as a central structuring device. More important, however, is their unanimous desire to affirm Native traditions and beliefs and survival. But as in the early novels of James Welch, another Montana writer, this affirmation of Native lifeways may not be obvious on the surface.

James Welch is of Blackfeet/Gros Ventre descent. His people are close neighbors of the Salish, and their verbal arts reflect a similar concern for the landscape of northern Montana. However, Welch's first two novels appear to be less concerned with Native subjects than those of his contemporaries: they do not employ direct references to or retellings of traditional stories, and their protagonists are effectively cut off from the traditions that provide identity and direction for their people. Yet each of these two novels relies very heavily upon motifs from the verbal arts, for each tells the story of a man on a journey of self-discovery in which he seeks to define his relationship with his land and his people. The journey motif is, of course, ubiquitous to all literatures and is therefore a useful structuring device for a novel that attempts to act as a bridge between two cultures, as McNickle learned.

In Welch's 1974 novel, *Winter in the Blood*, this bridge results in a comparison between two conflicting concepts of movement and, therefore, of ways of life. McNickle's vision of movement dating from the 1930s finds compelling expression in Welch's art. His protagonist's journey takes us through the traditional landscape of the Blackfeet, but it continually intersects with something new: the "Highline," or Highway 2, as it crosses northern Montana. The highway represents the imposition of European order and cultural attitudes, the same perceptions of the world presented in *The Surrounded* with the description of St. Xavier. And in each case, an alternative perception is offered.

On the Highline, the protagonist is at the mercy of forces beyond his control, forces that, like the gray elevator man in Havre, "take people up and down, whichever way they want to go."[2] As with all Natives since the incursion of the European, there seem to be no other alternatives: east/west, either/or, assimilate/die. And the Highline is a place of death. The protagonist's brother Mose and his father First Raise die on the highway, and he is beaten—physically, emotionally—on its course. The restrictions to movement and the death found on the Highline mark it as a place of evil, but one that is interestingly similar to those found in traditional Blackfeet verbal arts, where monsters inhabit places on trails that the Blackfeet must travel and where they prey upon the unwary.[3] Dangers such as these have always inhabited their pathways, and Blackfeet literature tells how to confront them. In many cases, the beings are inflexible; they perform the same predictable, evil actions time after time, and heroes use this inflexibility to destroy them, much as Coyote uses it in the Salish story of the Ram's Horn Tree. Like McNickle, Welch suggests that the old ways may still work. Appropriately, the protagonist's quest ends not on the highway, but in the tan land far away from the Highline's influence. It ends with the protagonist aware of his heritage and taking control of his life.

The quest of Jim Loney in Welch's second novel, *The Death of Jim Loney* (1979), also ends far from the main traveled roads. Here, however, the journey has been directed by forces other than the protagonist himself. He is guided by his instinctual responses to events, rather than by any self-motivated course of action. In short, he is moved by a vision, just as his Gros Ventre ancestors might have been moved, but Loney has no means of interpreting the vision of his "dark bird"—the Thunderbird called Bha'a in Gros Ventre literature.[4] He has had no education in how to respond appropriately, and the novel charts the ways that he is guided to the appropriate action—the working out of his vision. He becomes a warrior and a maker of storms, and the novel ends with Loney retreating into the mountains and taking a stand.[5] It is a bleak novel but, like its predecessor, it is ultimately an affirmation of ancient forces at work in the modern world and of a people's recognition and relationship with them. As Welch says in one interview, Loney's careful control over the events of his death is a creative act, and all creative acts are basically affirmative.[6]

In Welch's third novel, *Fools Crow* (1986), there is no attempt to mask tribal attitudes and arts. It carefully and elaborately describes a relationship between the Blackfeet, or more accurately the Pikuni, and their world. Set in the years from 1867 to 1870, it consistently depicts the interaction between characters (in particular Fools Crow) and forces in their world. These include Crow and Wolverine (animal mentors), the sun and morning star, and, most significantly, So-at-sa-ki (or Feather Woman) and Poia (Scar Face). In the book, characters from Blackfeet verbal arts converse and conspire with people of contemporary origin—and to good effect for their mutual world. Fools Crow and Crow rid the mountains of a crazy white man who kills animals merely for sport, and Fools Crow performs a vision quest which takes him to the sanctuary of So-at-sa-ki, a place at once physical and mythical, in which he is shown the future of his people.

The parallels between the writings of McNickle and Welch are obvious. *Fools Crow* echoes McNickle's interest in the "metaphysical" side of Native consciousness (found in the early drafts of *Wind from an Enemy Sky*) and his exploration of the origins of myth in *Runner in the Sun*. In both authors' works, motion plays a central role to illuminate the philosophical beliefs of a people and demonstrate appropriate, effective ways of cultural survival against compelling, destructive forces. But survival is always affirmed, despite apparent collapse and dissolution. *Fools Crow*, like *Wind*, has a bleak, yet qualified, conclusion. This is not to suggest that Welch was directly influenced by McNickle's earlier works but that they both possess a rich verbal heritage, recorded in both written and oral forms, and experiences with reservation life and tribal lifeways that influence both the subject matter of their art and its voice. This community of artistic endeavor extends beyond the northern plains and the two traditional enemies, the Blackfeet and Salish.

House Made of Dawn, by N. Scott Momaday (Kiowa), is perhaps the best known of contemporary Indian novels, and it reflects many of the concerns and strategies developed by McNickle. It traces the journey of a man from Jemez Pueblo as he attempts to understand his relationship with the land and his people, and the ways he must act in order to gain some means of control over his own life and future. It also contains characters from a variety of Native cultures: Tosamah the Kiowa, Benally the Navajo, Francisco, the Longhair from Jemez and an older generation. By telling of Abel's journey intersecting with theirs, Momaday demonstrates the concept that he sees as central to all Native cultures: the concept of "perfect motion." The most elaborate rendering of the concept in the novel focuses on Pueblo ceremonial practice, just as the Jemez story "The Emergence" (discussed in Chapter Three) focuses on the power of people's actions to work sweeping transformations in their world through ceremony. Like McNickle's description of the Dance and of Catharine's movements to prepare Narcisse for it, and Rafferty's insight about the Little Elk Indians' ways of moving, Momaday's novel emphasizes the obvious but seldom considered fact that a people's identity may be inextricably tied to the actions they perform and share as a community—continue the actions and the identity will endure. *House* ends, quite appropriately, with Abel participating in the dawn run—another less than obvious affirmation of tradition in modern times.

Momaday's use of Jemez traditions finds an interesting echo in the works of Leslie Marmon Silko who writes from another Pueblo culture, Laguna. In her first novel, *Ceremony*, she presents what must be, to date, the most intricately crafted attempt to render the associations between place and people, and the motions/actions through which they interact. She is, after all, Laguna and therefore fully aware of the stories of her people. Her writing, as well as her movies, reflects the richness found in Native verbal arts, which focus upon the relationship between mythic and historic, the past and the present. Her books emphatically and movingly present mythic characters who coexist with the contemporary, thus posing the question: "Are fiction and reality two distinct realms?"

Readers of *Ceremony* need to resolve that question, for Tayo's journey moves from the chaos of twentieth-century "reality" to a vision that brings order to the contemporary world through an awareness of the age-old pattern of powers in it. The similarities to themes found in McNickle's works are provocative, and the parallels between Archilde and Tayo, Tayo and Salt, are intriguing. In short, Tayo prevails despite acculturating influences, and he becomes a hero in the Laguna oral tradition, one who, like Salt in *Runner in the Sun*, provides his people with a new ceremony and power that will allow them to survive trying times.[7] By placing a traditional Laguna plot and character in a contemporary setting, Silko affirms the effectiveness of traditional ways to the knowledge of how to move and act, yet the ending of her novel does not have the potential for bleak misreading that the novels of McNickle, Welch, and Momaday possess. It clearly and unequivocally celebrates Laguna power of self-determination.

Gerald Vizenor, however, goes a step or two further. His novel, *Darkness in Saint Louis Bearheart*, stirs the emotions, and often the ire, of readers in ways suggestive of trickster. In fact, the novelist and the culture hero are perhaps inseparable, and usually to good effect. (For verification, watch his film *Harold of Orange*.) In his novel, Vizenor places a traditional Anishinaabeg (Chippewa/Ojibwa) hero on a traditional journey into the unknown territory of the west, but Vizenor sets that plot in the future, in a time after the earth's oil reserves have been depleted. Here there is no push for assimilation, at least in the ways we have been taught to define it. Instead, characters are compelled to adopt Indian ways. Once the oil is gone, chaos reigns along the highways of America. The American Dream dies, and American society takes to the countryside to survive. When groups try to maintain conventional social orders that were transitory because of their absolute reliance upon a limited, artificial resource, the results are ludicrous—mocking reflections of society today. Other emigrants from the cities and mainstream society turn tribal, but seldom to good effect.

However, Vizenor's protagonist, Proude Cedarfair, maintains order through his careful adherence to traditional ceremonial actions and thoughtful, well-considered reactions to the dangers, and temptations, he meets on the road to Chaco Canyon. It is a wonderfully surreal novel, for it places the reader on a journey through a specific landscape that may be traced on any map but in a mythical time that becomes increasingly difficult to relate to in any but a satirical sense. By introducing his readers to characters who are progressively more bizzare, thus gradually demanding more of the imagination, he can present traditional characters from Anishinaabeg verbal arts—such as the Evil Gambler and Thunderbird—in a way that makes them understandable by, and acceptable to, an uninitiated audience. They become credible because their surroundings and the other characters with whom we would compare them are incredible; they become alive because they become a possibility, a future, not products of a forgotten past. As a storyteller,

Vizenor provides the knowledge of how to act and react appropriately to the demands of the modern world, and he, engagingly and humorously, provides his audience with an affirmation of Native lifeways. Although a very different voice, his goals are those of McNickle.

These are only a very few of the powerful Native writers to be found today. Granted, they have been chosen for their notoriety and their exemplification of ideas and concepts relevant to McNickle's works, but they also represent the concern for an understanding of Native lifeways that motivates all Indian storytellers. Their subjects and approaches may vary owing to the differences in their backgrounds, but their desire to reach a general readership is universal, and their word ways share a similarity of effect predicated upon purpose and audience. Although it is impossible to gauge the effects McNickle may have had on their careers or their art, it can be safely assumed that he had an effect upon their readers.

When I began to wrestle with an analysis of the ways that McNickle's novels accomplish their goals, and the conclusions that may be drawn from them, an interesting thing happened. At the time, a local museum was exhibiting a collection of ancient Mimbres pottery; as I entered the well-lit hall with its carefully organized glass cases and soft brown colors, my mind was working on the problem that lay before me. How does McNickle demonstrate for his audience a different way of looking at this world? As I looked in the first case at a black and white clay form, I gave up trying to pry apart the knot in my thoughts, and I read the neatly typed card next to the bowl: "Winged Beings." I tried to see the beings in the design, but I could not. A series of triangular, black figures slanting down the bowl's interior provided the only pattern immediately recognizable. At the center, the bottom, there was a black ball that seemed to act as a head for them all, but there were no wings. I read the card again, and then looked back. It was the same.

I decided to give up and move on to the next case. As I did, the winged beings flew out at me. They were not black, but white. They existed in the spaces between the angular, geometrical, black, imposing figures that surrounded them. Yet, they both made up the bowl. There was a shock of recognition like the one felt when looking at those tricky pictures containing both a beautiful young woman with a full head of hair and an old witch with a big nose. The slightest shift in perception is all it takes to see both figures, and it cannot be forced. It comes when we are relaxed and receptive, when we let the figures emerge from their own backgrounds, and when we have learned that more than one perception is possible.

The novels work in much the same way. Their meanings emerge when we are prepared but refuse to impose preconceived forms on the stories they tell, when we allow them to move in the ways that they have moved for countless generations on this continent, and no doubt will continue to move for countless more thanks to Mc-Nickle and his successors, the Native writers of today. Through his efforts, primal Native attitudes have been transplanted from the spoken to the written narrative, and they reach a wide, nontribal audience. As he was quick to point out, Native peoples are, as always, changing, adapting to the circumstances of the contemporary world by employing new methods, and developing new ways to ensure cultural survival. As he notes in his preface to the 1975 edition of his book *They Came Here First*:

> The consequence of this development is that the venturing people who were the first to come into the New World and who adapted to its infinite variety may yet adapt to the conditions imposed by the competitive, acquisitive majority. But in adapting, by long experience, they will remain a separate and identifiable tradition, adding color to the fabric of American life.

This is true also of McNickle's life. His journey was enlightened by a vision he had as a young novelist, and it showed him what Native peoples needed to survive and prevail—without irreparable loss. Like much of American society, he originally believed tribes had lost or were losing their cultural identities as they abandoned old ways and beliefs to accept the ways of mainstream society. Through his work, he found just the opposite, and this revelation guided the efforts of a lifetime. A short time before his death, he once again voiced that understanding, an awareness that speaks to his own experience as well:

Indians might well insist that the sacred world was never abandoned, though the ceremonies honoring it may have lapsed or gone underground. Ethnologists doing field work in recent times have been surprised to discover that basic personality structures remain but little changed after generations of exposure to acculturating influences.[8]

"Ies choopminzin."

Appendix
Salish Oral Stories

Creation of the Red and White Races

Long, long ago when the world was young, Old Man in the Sky drained off the earth which he had made. When he had it crowded down into the big salt holes, the land became dry. About the same time, Old Man Coyote became lonely and so he went up into the Sky Land to talk to Old Man. Old Man questioned him.

"Why are you unhappy and crying? Have I not made much land for you to run about on? Are not Beaver, Otter, Bear, and Buffalo on the land to keep you company? Why do you not like Mountain Sheep? Did I not place him up in the hills, so that you need not fight? Why do you come up here so often, just to talk?"

Old Coyote sat down and cried many more tears. Old Man became very cross and began to scold. "Foolish old Coyote, you must not drop so much water upon the land. Have I not worked many days to dry it? Soon you will have it all covered with water again. What is the trouble with you? What more do you want to make you happy?"

"I am very lonely because I have no one to talk to," Coyote answered. "Beaver, Otter, Bear, and Buffalo are busy with their families. They do not have time to visit me. I want a people of my own, so that I may watch over them."

Old Man replied: "If you will stop this shedding of water, and stop annoying me with your visits, I will make you a people. Take this rawhide bag, this parfleche, and carry it to the mountain where there is red earth. Fill it full and bring it back to me. Hurry!"

Old Coyote took the bag and traveled many days and nights. Finally he came to a mountain where there was much red soil. Though weary after his long journey, he managed to fill the parfleche. Then he was sleepy.

"I will lie down to sleep for a while. When I awaken I will run swiftly back to Old Man in the Sky."

Coyote slept so soundly that he did not hear Mountain Sheep come along and look at the red soil in the bag.

"Foolish Coyote has come a long distance to get such a load of red soil," Mountain Sheep said to himself. "I wonder what he wants it for. I will have fun with him."

He dumped the red soil out upon the mountain. Then he filled the lower half of the bag with white earth and put some red soil on the upper half. Laughing to himself, Mountain Sheep ran away to his hiding place.

When Coyote awakened, he tied the top of the parfleche and hurried with it to Old Man in the Sky. The sun was going to sleep when he arrived. It was so dark that they could scarcely see the soil in the bag. Old Man in the Sky took the dirt and said, "I will make the soil into the forms of two men and two women."

He did not see that half the soil was red and half white.

"Take them to the dry land below," he said to Coyote when he had finished shaping them. "They are your people, and you can talk with them. So do not come up here to trouble me."

Old Coyote put the new people in the parfleche and carried them to dry land. In the morning when he took them out to put breath into them, he was surprised to find one pair red and the other pair white. Instantly he knew the trick that had been played upon him.

"I see that Mountain Sheep came while I slept," Coyote said. "What shall I do now? I know that I cannot keep these two colors together."

So he carried the white ones to the land by the big salt hole. The red ones he kept in his own land, so that he could visit with them.

That is how Indians and white men came upon the earth. And that is why Coyote was a friend of the Indians.

From Clark (1966, 73)

Amotken and Coyote

Amotken created Coyote to be his special helper, and assigned to him the welfare of all Indians. Coyote was to overcome the evil work of Amteep, the wicked chief of the lower world. Once Amteep tried to bring famine upon the earth by blighting the berries, fruits, and vegetables. So Coyote persuaded the salmon and the trout to seek places of spawning in the fresh-water streams, and he taught the Indians how to catch and prepare fish for food.

When Amteep emptied his parfleche, his rawhide bag containing diseases and illnesses, Coyote brought healing herbs from the upper world and planted them upon the earth. When the plants were ready for use, he taught the medicine men how to prepare them and how to use them in healing.

When Amotken saw that the people needed more food, he told

Coyote to bring buffalo to the plains, and to teach the Indians how to make bows and arrows and how to kill the great animals. Then Coyote showed them how to use the meat and the tallow. When Amteep blew his icy breath over the land to freeze the people, Coyote taught them to make clothing, bedding, and tipis from the warm robes of the buffalo.

During the early days, before Coyote was created, Amotken often appeared in person upon the earth, in order to teach the people to live better. Then he took the form of an elderly man, a white man. While Amotken was on the earth, there were no deaths, no suffering, no misfortunes of any kind. Winter did not come. Roots and fruits and berries were plentiful. Amteep and his evil helpers were unable to come up into the earth world.

"All people should live in peace," Amotken told the medicine men. "All men are brothers."

From Clark (1966, 68)

The Ram's Horn Tree

One day Coyote, after a long journey, was traveling up the Bitterroot Valley. Hungry and tired from his long trip, he paid little attention to where he was going. As he came near a big yellow pine tree, he heard a small voice cry out in pain, "Oh, you have broken my leg! It hurts terribly. When you stepped on me, I was about to tell you something important. Now I won't."

Fluttering around Coyote's feet was Meadow Lark. One leg was broken, and she was moaning in pain. Coyote felt sorry for her. Sitting down beside her, he said in a kind voice, "Stop crying. I will mend your leg so that it will be as good as ever."

He broke off some willow twigs and bound them on the bird's leg, wrapped the twigs with fine bark, and then rubbed the leg. With his powers, Coyote made the leg as good and strong as ever.

"Now that you are on your feet again," he said to Meadow Lark, "won't you tell me your secret?"

"Yes, I will. And thank you for healing my leg.

"This is what I planned to tell you. Not far from here lives a large mountain sheep, very powerful and very quick. You must not go farther, for the ram will hurt you if you do."

Coyote thought about Meadow Lark's warning for a while, but at last he decided to continue his journey. "I had better prepare myself to fight with the ram," he said within his heart. So he sang his power song and through his powers he got a magic flint knife.

"Now that sheep can not harm me," he said, as he started on, carrying his flint knife.

Almost at once he heard a great roaring sound. Looking up, he saw on a cliff above him a huge ram, pawing and snorting. Coyote decided to take his stand beside a big yellow pine. The ram surprised him by reaching the tree at the same time.

Coyote began to get a little worried. "What are you going to do to me?" he asked.

"I'm going to fight you. That's what I am going to do."

"Why?"

"Just because it is your turn," roared the ram. "I have fought everybody who has tried to come through this mountain pass. Now you are here, and it is your turn."

Coyote collected his wits and spoke calmly. "You must be very powerful. How do you fight? What are your weapons?"

"I *am* very powerful," answered the ram. "And I fight with my horns. With my sharp horns."

"Prove your power," said Coyote. "Prove your power first by striking this tree. Then you may do with me as you wish."

The mountain sheep was very proud of his strength and was very glad of his chance to show it. He stepped back a few feet, snorted a challenge to himself, and then charged at the tree at full speed. He struck it a few feet from the ground, struck it with such force that one of his horns passed entirely through the trunk.

While the ram was struggling to free himself, Coyote rushed forward, took out his knife, and cut off the head. The body fell to the ground. Then with just a touch of his flint knife, Coyote cut the head from the horns that were sticking through the tree. He picked up the head and hurled it across the valley against a high cliff. The blood of the ram splashed on the rock, and at once the face of a human being appeared on the cliff, looking toward the yellow pine tree.

Then Coyote made a prophecy: "This face on the cliff will be seen by generations to come. It will be a reminder of what has happened here. Many generations of people will pass this tree with the ram's horn in it, and it will become a wishing tree. If they will offer beads and feathers and moccasins, or this and that, and if they will make a wish with their offering, that wish will come true. They may wish for good luck or for food or for health—for anything they want—and it will be granted to them.

"If anyone makes a wish for ill luck, just to show off, that wish also will be granted, even if he asks for death."

And it came to pass even as Coyote prophesied. For many generations people passing through the Bitterroot Valley saw the face on the cliff and left their offerings with the tree. When I [Pierre Pichette] was a boy, the Indians gathered each summer at the Medicine Tree for ceremonial dances. They hung offerings on the tree and through it prayed to the Great Power for special benefits and blessings.

Years ago, a lumberjack tried to get the ram's horn out of the tree, but he could not. He did break off the point of the horn that had stuck out several inches beyond the bark.

From Clark (1966, 79)

Notes to the Chapters

Chapter 1. The Initiation: Fasting and Setting Out

1. See Clark (1966, 90).

2. Philomene McNickle, Letter to Superior Court, 8 April 1913, D'Arcy McNickle Papers, Newberry Library, Chicago. Note: the McNickle Papers are an uncataloged, loose collection of various writings: diaries, manuscripts, correspondence, etc.

3. Mother Superior of St. Ignatius School, Letter to Agent Morgan, 22 October 1914, D'Arcy McNickle Papers, Newberry Library, Chicago.

4. Philomene McNickle, Letter to Bureau of Indian Affairs, 2 November 1914, D'Arcy McNickle Papers, Newberry Library, Chicago.

5. "Letter to Constance Lindsay Skinner," 18 July 1935, McNickle Papers, Newberry Library, Chicago.

6. Fey and McNickle (1959, 110).

7. McKeehan (1983, 210).

8. An Early Vitae, McNickle Papers, Newberry Library, Chicago.

9. Ortiz (1979, 633).

10. In fact, Social Darwinism's theory of survival of the fittest has directed popular conceptions of progress and, therefore, colored attitudes about other cultures, including Native. A culture is "legitimate" only if it can conform to or withstand the onslaught of American social values, and governmental and economic systems. It is presumed that "primitive" cultures will conform and be assimilated because of the overpowering material attractiveness and strengths of the dominant culture. Such was the belief of those who initiated the federal boarding schools. See McKeehan (1983).

11. "Memorandum for the Press," McNickle Papers, Newberry Library, Chicago, 1. In this context, the faulty pronoun reference may be significant, for it may demonstrate McNickle's awareness of tribal unity; "its" may imply a communal, collective sense of identity, rather than an individual.

12. "Letter to John Collier," spring 1934, McNickle Papers, Newberry Library, Chicago.

13. Although the poem is quite romantic and Victorian in content and style, it is narrative—but narrative that does not work well. The short stories and novels, however, are narrative in which McNickle found a comfortable, rather than a contrived, voice. In particular, Mc-Nickle's papers contain the manuscript of a story dating from March 1935, entitled "Meat for God," that echoes, in a powerful, precise narrative, many of the contemporary concerns addressed in *The Surrounded*.

14. Charles Pearce, Letter to D'Arcy McNickle, 6 April 1929, Mc-Nickle Papers, Newberry Library, Chicago. It is important to note that Pearce and his reader betray the persistent attitude of the American public and publishers. He considers Indian and Black literatures as peripheral to the mainstream traditions of written narrative. Although in many ways distinct, they quite obviously evolve from the traditions of Western literature and should be considered as such.

15. "Diary Entry," 10 July 1931, McNickle Papers, Newberry Library, Chicago.

16. He fails to state, but the entry clearly suggests, that he may not lack maturity, in the usual sense of the word, but suffer instead from the confusion of two distinctly different social contexts. Recent scholars have recognized, and attempted to explain, the plight of Native children whose tribal conventions of communication became confused by those dictated in federal boarding schools. Although others have addressed this idea, Keith H. Basso's article, " 'To Give Up On Words': Silence in Western Apache" (1970, 213–20) is a telling exploration of children returning to the reservation after attending Indian Boarding Schools. McNickle's frustration was not his alone.

17. "Diary Entry," 15 July 1931, McNickle Papers, Newberry Library, Chicago.

18. *Report of the Commissioner of Indian Affairs* (1901).

19. "Diary Entry," 6 September 1930, McNickle Papers.

20. "Diary Entry," 9 October 1930, McNickle Papers.

21. "Diary Entry," 29 June 1932, McNickle Papers.

22. "Diary Entry," 16 September 1930, McNickle Papers.

23. "The Hungry Generations" MS, McNickle Papers, Newberry Library, Chicago, 2. All future references are to this manuscript; page numbers will be given in the text.

24. It is interesting that McNickle chose to describe Archilde's conversations as "story." Perhaps the idea of narrative was never distinctly separate from other types of discourse, at least in McNickle's mind.

25. The title, of course, possesses other implications derived from its use in Keats's "Ode." "The Hungry Generations" may be perceived as a disparaging image of McNickle's own people: the destitute generations

that have stifled those who wish to soar or sing. Perhaps it reflects McNickle's ambivalent attitudes about his people at this point in his life. (Late discussion of the manuscript addresses this possibility.)

26. Silko (1979, 211–16). Hobson (1981, 100–8) adds his own comments on the subject: "Quite simply, I believe Indian people are growing tired of the Oliver LaFarges and Jerome Rothenbergs speaking for them. . . ."

27. "Letter to William Gates," 25 March 1934, McNickle Papers, Newberry Library, Chicago.

28. Ibid.

29. "Letter to Marius Barbeau," 14 July 1935, McNickle Papers, Newberry Library, Chicago.

30. "Letter to Constance Lindsay Skinner," 6 October 1935, McNickle Papers, Newberry Library, Chicago.

31. For a discussion of the Foolish Folk, see Turney-High (1941, 15–17), who records a story about them.

32. Clark (1966, 66–68). It must be noted that Clark's work was chosen because she, quite by accident, compiled stories from several sources which, mysteriously (and fortuitously for this study), seem to have affected McNickle also. "In the Beginning," the origin story, was collected originally by Father Gregory Mengarini, who assisted De-Smet; "Amotken and Coyote" came from informants on the reservation of McNickle's youth; and Alexander Ross records the existence of The Ram's Horn Tree.

33. Clark (1966, 68).

34. Clark (1966, 80).

Chapter 2. The Vision

1. "The Hungry Generations" MS, McNickle Papers, Newberry Library, Chicago, 338.

2. Ibid., 302.

3. Ibid., 301.

4. Covici, Friede, Inc., Letter to D'Arcy McNickle, 23 October 1934, McNickle Papers, Newberry Library, Chicago.

5. Contract for Publication of "Dead Grass," 29 October 1934, McNickle Papers, Newberry Library, Chicago.

6. D'Arcy McNickle (1978, 21). All future references are to this edition; pagination will be given in the text.

7. Compare this motif with that found in the story Clark entitles "In the Beginning," collected by Father Mengarini, one of the first priests to meet the Salish.

8. Fahey (1974, 71).

9. Turney-High (1941, 50).

10. "Letter to William Gates," 25 March 1934, McNickle Papers, Newberry Library, Chicago.

11. "Letter to E. H. Dodd, Jr.," 2 January 1936, McNickle Papers, Newberry Library, Chicago.

12. Fahey (1974, 65).

13. "Letter to William Gates," 26 July 1934, McNickle Papers, Newberry Library, Chicago.

14. Sanders (1910, 22–25).

15. "Letter to Ruth Rae," 28 November 1935, McNickle Papers, Newberry Library, Chicago.

16. Indeed, a great deal of scholarly work has been done recently in this area. In particular, scholars such as Dell Hymes, Dennis Tedlock, Jarold Ramsey, Elaine Jahner, Barre Toelken, and Kathleen Sands have worked to enlighten the dynamics of oral storytelling and to apply knowledge of its nature to the writings of contemporary Native authors.

17. "Letter to Marius Barbeau." 14 July 1935, McNickle Papers, Newberry Library, Chicago.

18. Barbeau (1923, 68).

19. One finds similar attitudes in the writings of Leslie Silko, James Welch, Gerald Vizenor, N. Scott Momaday, and Louise Erdrich, to name only a few.

20. The "Memorandum for the Press" cited in Chapter One conveys this idea quite forcefully, emphatically.

21. For discussions of the Sun Dance, see Clark (1966, 68) or Johnson (1969, 19–24).

22. Barbeau, 172.

23. Ibid., 173.

24. For a full discussion of McWhorter's intrusions and an explication of Mourning Dove's dilemma, see Brown (1988, 2–15).

25. D'Arcy McNickle (1971, 56).

26. This quotation is from the manuscript "The Hungry Generations."

27. Larson (1978, 77).

28. Owens (1985).

29. Ruth Rae, Letter to D'Arcy McNickle, 4 March 1936, McNickle Papers, Newberry Library, Chicago .

30. J. Verne Dusenberry, Letter to D'Arcy McNickle, 30 March 1936, McNickle Papers, Newberry Library, Chicago.

31. J. Verne Dusenberry, Letter to D'Arcy McNickle, 3 June 1936, McNickle Papers, Newberry Library, Chicago. (Note also the reference to Dusenberry in the bibliography.)

32. "Invoice, Royalty Payments," 1 August 1936, McNickle Papers, Newberry Library, Chicago.

33. Vorse (1936, 295–96).

34. Milner (1936, 3).

35. La Farge (1936, 10).

36. "Letter to Richard Pope," 15 March 1975, McNickle Papers, Newberry Library, Chicago.

Chapter 3.   The Journey to the South

1. Ortiz (1987, 248).

2. Field Notebooks, 1 June 1950, McNickle Papers, Newberry Library, Chicago.

3. In his afterword to the 1987 edition of *Runner*, Ortiz retells one of McNickle's favorite anecdotes—about a Cree student who makes a journey retracing Salt's. Ortiz also provides a valuable discussion of the historical events that may have influenced McNickle's pantribal approach, including the termination act of the year *Runner* was published.

4. "The Boy Who Stole the Sun" MS, McNickle Papers, Newberry Library, Chicago.

5. Parsons (1925, 136).

6. References to this pattern of convergence and then emergence can be found in the works of Applegate (1979), Boas (1917, 1925), Coffer (1978), and Gunn (1917). It is also addressed in the context of modern fiction in "An Act of Attention: Event Structure in *Ceremony*" (Jahner, 1979, 37–46).

7. Parsons (1925, 137).

8. The concept of "perfect motion" as presented in "The Emergence" is explored fully in N. Scott Momaday's award-winning novel *House Made of Dawn* (1968), which is also set in Jemez.

9. D'Arcy McNickle (1954, 52). All future references are to this edition; pagination will be given in the text.

Chapter 4.   A Vision of Movement

1. D'Arcy McNickle, "Information About Your Writing," 27 November 1976, from Harper & Row files, San Francisco.

2. Ibid.

3. "Letter to Alain Henon," 16 June 1977, McNickle Papers, Newberry Library, Chicago.

4. "Snowfall" MS, McNickle Papers, Newberry Library, Chicago, 13.

5. Ibid., 17.

6. "Indian Agent" MS, McNickle Papers, Newberry Library, Chicago, 380.

7. Ibid.,

8. Ibid., 399.

9. Ibid., 402.

10. "Letter," 7 December 1969, McNickle Papers, Newberry Library, Chicago.

11. "Letter to Elaine Edleman," 27 August 1974, McNickle Papers, Newberry Library, Chicago.

12. "Indian Agent" MS, 22.

13. D'Arcy McNickle, *Wind from an Enemy Sky* (1978, 1). All future references are to this edition; pagination will be given in the text.

14. "Information" from Harper & Row.

15. D'Arcy McNickle, *The Surrounded* (1978, 215).

16. "Letter to Alain Henon."

17. The Museum of the American Indian still faces the problems McNickle witnessed in the 1930s and 1940s. See Grimes (1988).

18. Letter received from Robert D. San Souci, 21 November 1984.

Chapter 5.   The Vision Today

1. Perhaps the criticism of these works and other works by Native artists should also emerge from the tribal cultures that produce them. Since the audience for criticism, like the audience for fiction, is well versed in the conventions of Euramerican culture, analyses or explications should work to enlighten the ways that Native perceptions and means of expression animate and enhance the written by beginning with the verbal arts and working outward.

2. Welch (1974, 121).

3. Such stories can be found in the works of George Bird Grinnell, Walter McClintock, and, most recently, Percy Bullchild.

4. For discussions of Bha'a, see Flannery (1956).

5. See Sands (1980, 61–78) and Purdy (1987, 17–24).

6. Bevis (1982, 169–85).

7. Purdy (1987, 121–33).

8. "Letter to Alain L. Henon," 16 June 1977, McNickle Papers, Newberry Library, Chicago.

Bibliography

Adamson, Thelma, ed. *Folk-Tales of the Coast Salish*. New York: American Folklore Society, 1934.

Allen, Paula Gunn. "Symbol and Structure in Native American Literature: Some Basic Considerations." *College Composition and Communication*, 24 (1973), 267–70.

————. "The Mythopoetic Vision in Native American Literature." *American Indian Culture and Research Journal*. 1 (1974), 3–13.

Applegate, Frank G. *Indian Stories from the Pueblos: Tales of New Mexico and Arizona*. 1929; rpt. Glorieta, N.M., 1979.

Astov, Margot. "The Concept of Motion as the Psychological Leit-Motif of Navajo Life and Literature." *Journal of American Folklore*, 63 (1950), 45–56.

Ballinger, Franchot. "The Responsible Center: Man and Nature in Pueblo and Navajo Songs and Prayers." *American Quarterly*, 30, 90–107.

Barbeau, Marius. *Indian Days in the Canadian Rockies*. Toronto: Macmillan, 1923.

Barthes, Roland. *Image-Music-Text*. New York: Hill and Wang, 1977.

Bascom, William R. "Folklore and Anthropology." *Journal of American Folklore*, 66 (1953), 283–90.

Basso, Keith H. " 'To Give Up On Words': Silence in Western Apache." *Southwestern Journal of Anthropology*, 26:3 (Autumn 1970), 213–20.

Bataille, Gretchen. "American Indian Literature: Traditions and Translations." *Melus*, 6, No. 4 (Winter 1979), pp. 17–26.

Bauer, George W. "Cree Tales and Beliefs." *Northeast Folklore*, 12 (1971), 1–70.

Beidler, Peter G. "Animals and Human Development in the Contemporary American Indian Novel." *Western American Literature*, 14:2 (Summer 1979), 133–48.

Ben-Amos, Dan, ed. *Folklore: Performance and Communication*. The Hague: 1975.

————, ed. *Folklore Genres*. Austin: Univ. of Texas Press, 1976.

Bevis, Bill. "Dialogue with James Welch." *Northwest Review*, 20 (1982), 163–85.

Bierhorst, John. "American Indian Verbal Art and the Literary Critic." *Journal of American Folklore*, 88 (1975), 402–8.

Boas, Franz. *Folk-Tales of the Salishan and the Sahaptin Tribes*. New York: American Folklore Society, 1917.

———. *Keresan Texts*. New York: American Ethnological Society, 1925.

Booth, Wayne. *The Rhetoric of Fiction*. 2nd ed. Chicago: Univ. of Chicago Press, 1983.

Brown, Alanna Kathleen. "Mourning Dove's Voice in *Cogewea*." *The Wicazo Sa Review*, 4:2 (Spring 1988), 2–15.

Brumble, H. David III. "Anthropologists, Novelists and Indian Sacred Material." *Canadian Review of American Studies*, 11:1 (Spring 1980), 31–48.

Buller, Galen. "New Interpretations of Native American Literature: A Survival Technique." *American Indian Culture and Research Journal*, 4:1&2 (1980), 165–77.

Capps, Walter H. *Seeing with the Native Eye: Essays on Native American Religion*. New York: Harper & Row, 1976.

Chapman, Abraham, ed. *Literature of the American Indians: Views and Interpretations*. New York: New American Library, 1975.

Chatman, Seymore. *Story and Discourse: Narrative Structure in Fiction and Film*. Ithaca, N.Y.: Cornell University Press, 1978.

Clark, Ella E. *Indian Legends from the Northern Rockies*. Norman: University of Oklahoma Press, 1966.

———, ed. "Northwest Indian Coyote Tales." *Northwest Review*, 6 (Summer 1963), 21–36.

Coffer, William E. *Spirits of the Sacred Mountains: Creation Stories of the American Indian*. Florence, Kentucky: Van Nostrand, 1978.

Collier, John. *Indians of the Americas: The Long Hope*. New York: Mentor Books, 1948.

Culler, Jonathan D. *The Pursuit of Signs: Semiotics, Literature, Deconstruction*. Ithaca, N.Y.: Cornell University Press, 1981.

Davis, Jack L. "The Whorf Hypothesis and Native American Literature." *South Dakota Review*, 14:ii, 59–72.

Dorris, Michael. "Native American Literature in an Ethnohistorical Context." *College English*, 41:2 (October 1979), 147–62.

Dusenberry, Verne. *The Montana Cree: A Study in Religious Persistence*. Stockholm: Almquist & Wiksell, 1962.

Fahey, John. *The Flathead Indians*. Norman: Univ. of Oklahoma Press, 1974.

Fey, Harold E., and D'Arcy McNickle. *Indians and Other Americans: Two Ways of Life Meet*. New York: Harper & Brothers, 1959.

Fitzgerald, Helen Sanders. *Trails Through Western Woods.* New York: Alice Harriman Co., 1910.

Flannery, Regina. *The Gros Ventre of Montana.* Harlem, Montana: Gros Ventre Treaty Committee, 1956.

Georges, Robert A. "Toward an Understanding of Storytelling Events." *Journal of American Folklore,* 82 (1969), 313–28.

Gill, Sam. *Native American Religions: An Introduction.* Belmont, Calif.: Wadsworth Publishing Co., 1982.

Grimes, William. "The Indian Museum's Last Stand." *New York Times Magazine.* 27 November 1988, 46+.

Grinnell, George Bird. *Blackfoot Lodge Tales: The Story of a Prairie People.* Lincoln: Univ. of Nebraska Press, 1962.

Gunn, John M. *Schat-chen: History, Traditions and Narratives of the Queres Indians of Laguna and Acoma.* Albuquerque, N.M.: Albright & Anderson, 1917.

Hobson, Geary S., ed. "The Rise of the White Shaman as a New Version of Cultural Imperialism." *The Remembered Earth: An Anthology of Contemporary Native American Literature.* Albuquerque: Univ. of New Mexico Press, 1981. 100–8.

Hymes, Dell. "Discovering Oral Performance and Measured Verse in American Indian Narratives." *New Literary History,* 8 (1976–77), 439–57.

———. "The Grounding of Performance and Text in a Narrative View of Life." *Alcheringa,* 4:1 (1978), 137–40.

Iser, Wolfgang. *The Act of Reading: A Theory of Aesthetic Response.* Baltimore: Johns Hopkins University Press, 1978.

Jahner, Elaine. "An Act of Attention: Event Structure in *Ceremony.*" *American Indian Quarterly,* 5:1 (1979), 37–46.

———. "Critical Approaches to Contemporary American Indian Literature." *Studies in American Indian Literatures,* 2:1 (Spring 1978), 6–7.

Johnson, Olga Weydemeyer. *Flathead and Kootenay: The Rivers, The Tribes and the Region's Traders.* Glendale, California: Arthur H. Clark Co., 1969.

Kroeber, A. L. *Ethnology of the Gros Ventre.* Anthropological Papers of the American Museum of Natural History, Vol. I, Part IV, 1908.

———. *Gros Ventre Myths and Tales.* Anthropological Papers of the American Museum of Natural History, Vol. I, Part III, 1907.

Kroeber, Karl. "Deconstructionist Criticism and American Indian Literature." *Boundary 2,* 7:3 (Spring 1979), 73–89.

———, ed. *Traditional Literatures of the American Indian: Texts and Interpretations.* Lincoln: Univ. of Nebraska Press, 1981.

Krupat, Arnold. "An Approach to Native American Texts." *Critical Inquiry,* 9:ii (December 1983), 323–38.

———. "Native American Literature and the Canon." *Critical Inquiry,* 10:i (September 1983), 145–71.

La Farge, Oliver. "Half-Breed Hero." *Saturday Review of Literature.* March 14, 1936, 10.

———. *Laughing Boy.* Greenport, New York: Harmony Raine & Co., 1981. Originally published in 1929.

Larson, Charles R. *American Indian Fiction.* Albuquerque: Univ. of New Mexico Press, 1978.

Lattin, Vernon E. "The Quest for Mythic Vision in Contemporary Native American and Chicano Fiction." *American Literature,* 50 (1979), 625–40.

Lemon, Lee T., and Marion J. Reis, eds. *Russian Formalists.* Lincoln: Univ. of Nebraska Press, 1965.

Lincoln, Kenneth. *Native American Renaissance.* Berkeley: Univ. of California Press, 1984.

McClintock, Walter. *The Old Trail or Life, Legends and Religion of the Blackfeet Indians.* Lincoln: Univ. of Nebraska Press, 1968.

McKeehan, Patrick Michael. *The History of Chemawa Indian School.* Ann Arbor, Michigan: University Microfilms International, 1983.

McNickle, D'Arcy. "Information About Your Writing." From Harper & Row Files, San Francisco.

———. D'Arcy McNickle Papers. Newberry Library, Chicago.

———. *Indian Man: A Life of Oliver La Farge.* Bloomington: Indiana University Press, 1972.

———. *Indians and Other Americans.* New York: Harper & Row, 1959.

———. *Native American Tribalism: Indian Survival and Renewals.* New York: Oxford University Press, 1973.

———. *Runner in the Sun: A Story of Indian Maize.* New York: Holt, Rinehart & Winston, 1954.

———. *The Surrounded.* Albuquerque: Univ. of New Mexico Press, 1978.

———. *They Came Here First.* New York: Harper & Row, 1975.

———. *Wind from an Enemy Sky.* New York: Harper & Row, 1978.

Milner, Florence. "A Novel of the Mountain Indian." *Boston Transcript.* March 4, 1936, 3.

Momaday. N. Scott. *House Made of Dawn.* New York: Harper & Row, 1968.

Nabokov, Peter. "American Indian Literature: A Tradition of Renewal." *Studies of American Indian Literatures,* 2:3 (Autumn 1978), 31–40.

Oaks, Priscilla. "Native American Novelists of the Thirties." *Melus,* 5:1 (Spring 1978), 57–65.

Ortiz, Alfonso. Obituary for D'Arcy McNickle. *American Anthropologist.* 81:3 (Sept. 1979), 632–36.

————. "Afterword." *Runner in the Sun: A Story of Indian Maize*. By D'Arcy McNickle. Albuquerque: Univ. of New Mexico Press, 1987. 248.

Owens, Louis. "The Map of the Mind: D'Arcy McNickle and the American Indian Novel." *Western American Literature*, 19:4 (Winter 1985), 275–83.

Parsons, Elsie Clews. *Pueblo Indian Religion*. Chicago: Univ. of Chicago Press, 1939.

————. *The Pueblo of Jemez*. New Haven: Yale University Press, 1925.

Purdy, John Lloyd. "Bha'a and *The Death of Jim Loney*." *Studies in American Indian Literatures*, 11:1 (Winter 1987), 17–24.

————. "The Transformation: Tayo's Genealogy in *Ceremony*." *Studies in American Indian Literatures*, 10:3 (Summer 1986), 121–33.

Ramsey, Jarold. *Reading the Fire: Essays in the Traditional Indian Literatures of the Far West*. Lincoln: Univ. of Nebraska Press, 1983.

————. "Word Magic." *Parnassus*, 4:i, 165–75.

Report of the Commissioner of Indian Affairs 1901. Washington: U.S. Government Printing Office, 1901.

Rimmon-Kenan, Shlomith. *Narrative Fiction*. New York: Methuen, 1983.

Ruppert, James. *D'Arcy McNickle*. Boise: Western Writers Series, 1988.

Sands, Kathleen Mullen. "*The Death of Jim Loney*: Indian or Not?" *Studies in American Indian Literatures*, 7:1 (Spring 1980), 61–78.

Sanders, Helen Fitzgerald. *Trails Through Western Woods*. New York: Alice Harriman Co., 1910.

Sanders, Thomas E. "Tribal Literature: Individual Identity and the Collective Unconscious." *College Composition and Communication*, 24 (1973), 256–66.

San Souci, Robert D. Letter to the Author. November 21, 1984.

Schneider, Jack W. "The New Indian: Alienation and the Rise of the Indian Novel." *South Dakota Review*, 17 (Winter 1979–80). 67–76.

Sealy, D. Bruce, and Antoine S. Lussier. *The Métis: Canada's Forgotten People*. Winnepeg: Pemmican Publications, 1975.

Silko, Leslie Marmon. *Ceremony*. New York: Viking Press, 1977.

————. "An Old Time Indian Attack Conducted in Two Parts." *The Remembered Earth: An Anthology of Contemporary Native American Literature*. Ed. Geary S. Hobson. Albuquerque: Univ. of New Mexico Press, 1981. 211–16.

Skinner, Alamonsa. "Plains Cree Tales." *Journal of American Folklore*, 29 (1916), 341–67.

Swan, Brian, ed. *Smoothing the Ground: Essays on Native American Oral Literature*. Berkeley: Univ. of California Press, 1983.

Swindlehurst, Fred. "Folk-Lore of the Cree Indians." *Journal of American Folklore*, 18 (1905), 139–43.

Tedlock, Dennis. "On the Translation of Style in Oral Narrative." *Journal of American Folklore*, 84 (Jan.–March 1971), 114–33.

———. "Toward an Oral Poetics." *New Literary History*, 8 (1976–77), 507–18.

Toelken, Barre. *The Dynamics of Folklore*. New York: Houghton Mifflin, 1979.

Turney-High, Henry Holbert. *The Flathead Indians of Montana*. Menasha, Wisconsin: Memoirs of the Anthropological Association, Vol. 43, No. 2, Part 2, 1941.

Vizenor, Gerald. *Darkness in Saint Louis Bearheart*. Saint Paul, Minnesota: Truck Press, 1978.

Vorse, Mary Heaton. "End of the Trail." *The New Republic*. April 15, 1936, 295–96.

Welch, James. *The Death of Jim Loney*. New York: Harper & Row, 1979.

———. *Winter in the Blood*. New York: Harper & Row, 1974.

———. *Fool's Crow*. New York: Viking, 1986.

Weisel, George P. "A Flathead Indian Tale." *Journal of American Folklore*, 65 (1952), 359–60.

Wilson, Norma. "Outlook for Survival." *Denver Quarterly*, 14:4 (Winter 1980), 22–30.

Index

Verbal arts, xii, xiv, 9, 11, 54–55,
91, 133, 138; *in medias res,* 14;
in *Runner,* 87, 96; in *Surrounded,*
23–33, 40, 56, 58
Village of the White Rocks (*Runner*), 87, 88, 93, 103
Vision quest, 137; of Archilde, 35–
37, 39, 52, 71, 74; of D'Arcy
McNickle, xiv, 5, 11–13, 19,
141–42. *See also* Journey;
Knowledge, ways to
Vizenor, Gerald, *Darkness in Saint
Louis Bearheart,* 139–40
Vorse, Mary Heaton, 79

*Wah'Kon-Tah: The Osage and the
White Man's Road* (Mathews), 67
Welch, James, 135; *Death of Jim
Loney, The,* 136; *Fools Crow,* 136–
37; *Winter in the Blood,* 135–36
White House (Canyon de Chelly),

87, 91
Wind from an Enemy Sky
(McNickle), xiii, 67, 106–33,
134, 137, 138; anger in, 116–
17, 126–27, 129, 132; autobiographical elements in, 107,
118, 119, 124; compared with
Runner, 109, 121; compared
with *Surrounded,* 109–10, 113–
15, 117, 119, 121, 126, 129,
132; discussion of conclusion,
132–33; origins of, 106–7;
songs in, 111–12, 121–23, 124–
25, 132. *See also* Antoine; Boy,
The; Bull; Dam (in *Wind*); Fatalism, in *Wind*; Henry Jim; Pell,
Adam; Perceptions, two (Native
vs. Anglo); Plots, two (Native vs.
Anglo); Rafferty, Indian Agent;
"Snowfall"
Winter in the Blood (Welch), 135–
36